Through
The Eyez of Mine

Aaron Grossman

Dedicated to My Mum
Margaret Mary Marjoram
(in loving memory of Trevor "SLY" Dailey)

Contents

CHAPTER ONE

Welcome, 2 Manchester.
The Mancunian Way.

Towering over Old Trafford, the Seven Sisters may have looked like just another set of old council housing blocks – but to their first residents 50 years ago, they felt like paradise. Built-in the 1960s as part of a project to clear Manchester's slums, the towers have now taken on new poignancy as four have now been demolished.

The remaining three – Clifford Court, Grafton Court and Pickford Court – have had a £12m refurbishment by Trafford Housing Trust.

Manchester is a city and metropolitan borough in Greater Manchester England. The city has the country's fifth-largest population at 547,627 (as of 2018) and lies within the United Kingdom's second-most populous urban area with a population of 2.7 million, third most populous, at around 2.8 million, and a third-most populous metropolitan area with a population of 3.3 million.

It is fringed by the Cheshire Plain to the south, the Pennines to the north and east, and an arc of towns with which it forms a continuous conurbation. The local authority for the city is the Manchester City council.

The recorded history of Manchester began with the civilian settlement associated with the Roman fort of Mamucium or Mancunium, which was established in about AD 79 on a sandstone bluff near the confluence of the rivers Medlock and Irwell.

Although historically and traditionally a part of Lancashire, areas of Cheshire south of the River Mersey were incorporated into Manchester in the 20th century. The first to be included, Wythenshawe, was added to the city in 1931. Throughout the Middle Ages Manchester remained a manorial township but began to expand "at an astonishing rate "around the turn of the 19th century. Manchester's unplanned urbanisation was brought on by a boom in textile manufacture during the industrial revolution and resulted in it becoming the world's first industrialised city.

Manchester achieved its city's status in 1853. The Manchester ship canal opened in 1894, creating the Port of Manchester and directly linking the city to the Irish Sea, 36 miles (58 km) to the west.

Its fortune declined after the Second World War owing to deindustrialisation, but the IRA bombing in 1996 led to extensive investment and regeneration.

Following successful redevelopment after the IRA bombing, Manchester was the host city for the 2002 commonwealth games which helped the English economy grow massively since the 1996 IRA bombing.

The city is notable for its architecture, culture, musical exports, media links, scientific & engineering output, social impact, sports clubs and transport connections. Manchester Liverpool Road railway station was the world's first inter-city passenger railway station.

ETYMOLOGY.

The name Manchester originates from the Latin name Mamucium or its variant Mancunio and the citizens are still referred to as Mancunians. These names are generally thought to represent a Latinisation of an original Brittonic name. The generally accepted etymology of this name is that it comes from Brittonic *mamm- ("breast", about a "breast-like hill"). However, more recent work suggests that it could come from *mamma ("mother", about a local river goddess). Both usages are preserved in Insular Celtic languages, such as mam meaning "breast" in Irish and "mother" in Welsh. The suffix Chester is from Old English ceaster ("Roman fortification", itself a loanword from Latin castra, "fort; a fortified town"

MANCHESTER'S EARLY HISTORY.

The Brigantes were the major Celtic tribe in what is now known as Northern England; they had a stronghold in the locality at a sandstone outcrop on which Manchester Cathedral now stands, opposite the bank of the River Irwell.

Their territory extended across the fertile lowland of what is now Salford and Stretford. Following the Roman conquest of Britain in the 1st century, General Agricola ordered the construction of a fort named Mamucium in the year 79 to ensure that Roman interests in Deva Victrix (Chester) and Eboracum (York) were protected from the Brigantes.

Central Manchester has been permanently settled since this time. A stabilised fragment of foundations of the final version of the Roman fort is visible in Castlefield. The Roman habitation of Manchester probably ended around the 3rd century; its civilian settlement appears to have been abandoned by the mid-3rd century, although the fort may have supported a small garrison until the late 3rd or early 4th century. After the Roman withdrawal and Saxon conquest, the focus of settlement shifted to the confluence of the Irwell and Irk sometime before the arrival of the Norman's after 1066.

Much of the wider area was laid waste in the subsequent harrying of the north.

Dating back times from the era of 1065 Manchester is recorded as within the hundred of Salford and held as a tenant in chief by a Norman named (Roger of Poitou), later being held by the family of Greeley, lord of the manor and residents of Manchester council until 1215 before a Manor House was built.

By 1421 Thomas de la Warre founded and constructed a collegiate church for the parish, now Manchester cathedral; the domestic premises of the college house Chetham's school of music & Chetham's library. The library, which opened in 1653 and is still open to the public today, is the oldest free public reference library in the United Kingdom.

Manchester is mentioned as having a market in 1282. Around the 14th century, Manchester received an influx of Flemish weavers, sometimes credited as the foundation of the region's textile industry.

Manchester became an important centre for the manufacture and trade of woollens & linen, and by about 1540, had expanded to become, in John Talend's words,

"The fairest, best built, quickest, and most populous town of all Lancashire. "The cathedral and Chetham's buildings are the only significant survivors of Leland's Manchester.

During the English civil war, Manchester strongly favoured the Parliamentary interest. Although not long-lasting, Cromwell granted it the right to elect its MP, (Charles Worsley) who sat for the city for only a year, was later appointed Major General for Lancashire, Cheshire and Staffordshire during the Rule of the major general's. He was a diligent puritan, turning out ale houses and banning the celebration of Christmas; he died in 1656.

Significant quantities of cotton began to be used after about 1600, firstly in linen/cotton fustians, but by around 1750 pure cotton fabrics were being produced and cotton had overtaken wool in importance. The Irwell and Mersey were made navigable by 1736, opening a route from Manchester to the sea docks on the Mersey. The Bridgewater Canal, Britain's first wholly artificial waterway, was opened in 1761, bringing coal from mines at Worsley to central Manchester. The canal was extended to the Mersey at Runcorn by 1776. The combination of competition and improved efficiency halved the cost of coal and halved the transport cost of raw cotton.

Manchester became the dominant marketplace for textiles produced in the surrounding towns. A commodities exchange opened in 1729, and numerous large warehouses, aided commerce. In 1780, Richard Arkwright began the construction of Manchester's first cotton mill. In the early 1800s, John Dalton formulated his atomic theory in Manchester.

INDUSTRIAL REVOLUTION.

Manchester was one of the centres of textile manufacturers during the industrial revolution. The great majority of cotton spinning took place in the towns of south Lancashire and north Cheshire, and Manchester was for a time the most productive centre of cotton processing.

Manchester became known as the world's largest marketplace for cotton goods and was dubbed "Cottonoplois" and "Warehouse City" during the Victorian Era. In Australia, New Zealand and South Africa, the term "manchester" is still used for household linen: sheets, pillowcases, towels, etc.

The industrial revolution brought about a huge change in Manchester and was key to the increase in Manchester's growing population.

Manchester began expanding "at an astonishing rate" around the turn of the 19th century as people flocked to the city for work from Scotland, Wales, Ireland and other areas of England as part of a process of unplanned urbanisation brought on by the Industrial revolution It developed a wide range of industries, so that by 1835 "Manchester was without challenge the first and greatest industrial city in the world." Engineering firms initially made machines for the cotton trade but diversified into general manufacture. Similarly, the chemical industry started by producing bleaches and dyes but expanded into other areas. Commerce was supported by financial service industries such as banking and insurance.

Trade, and feeding the growing population, required a large transport and distribution infrastructure: the canal system was extended, and Manchester became one end of the world's first intercity passenger railway—the Liverpool and Manchester Railway. Competition between the various forms of transport kept costs down. In 1878 the G.P.O the (General Post Office) (the forerunner of British Telecom) provided its first telephones to a firm in Manchester.

The Manchester ship canal was built between 1888 and 1894, in some sections by canalisation of the Rivers Irwell and Mersey, running 36 miles (58 km) from Salford to Eastham Locks on the tidal Mersey. This enabled ocean-going ships to sail right into the Port of Manchester. On the canal's banks, just outside the borough, the world's first industrial estate was created at Trafford Park.

Large quantities of machinery, including cotton processing plants, were exported around the world.

A centre of capitalism, Manchester was once the scene of bread and labour riots, as well as calls for greater political recognition by the city's working and non-titled classes. One such gathering ended with the Peterloo Massacre of 16 August 1819. The Peterloo Massacre took place at St Peter's Field, Manchester, Lancashire, England on Monday 16 August 1819. Eighteen people died when cavalry charged into a crowd of around 60,000 people who had gathered to demand the reform of parliamentary representation.

The economic school of Manchester capitalism developed there, and Manchester was the centre of the Anticorn law league from 1838 onward.

Manchester has a notable place in the history of Marxism and left-wing politics; being the subject of Friedrich Engels' work (The condition of the working class of people in England 1844.) which I recommend for those in search of history; Engels spent much of his life in and around Manchester, and when Karl Marx visited Manchester, they met at Chetham's Library. The economics books Marx was reading at the time can be seen in the library, as can the window seat where Marx and Engels would meet. The first Trades union congress was held in Manchester (at the Mechanics' Institute, David Street), from 2 to 6 June 1868 my birthday month.

Manchester was an important cradle of the Labour Party and the Suffragette Movement. At that time, it seemed a place in which anything could happen—new industrial processes, new ways of thinking (the Manchester School, promoting free trade and (laiszze faith), new classes or groups in society, new religious sects, and new forms of labour organisation. It attracted educated visitors from all parts of Britain and Europe. A saying capturing this sense of innovation survives today: "What Manchester does today, the rest of the world does tomorrow.

"Manchester's golden age was perhaps the last quarter of the 19th century.

Many of the great public buildings (including Manchester Town Hall) date from then. The city's cosmopolitan atmosphere contributed to a vibrant culture, which included the Hallè orchestra. In 1889, when county councils were created in England, the municipal borough became a county borough with even greater autonomy.

Although the Industrial Revolution brought wealth to the city, it also brought poverty and squalor to a large part of the population. History shows "Manchester was the very best and the very worst taken to terrifying extremes, a new kind of city in the world; the chimneys of industrial suburbs greeting you with columns of smoke". An American visitor taken to Manchester's blackspots saw "wretched, defrauded, oppressed, crushed human nature, lying and bleeding fragments".

The number of cotton mills in Manchester itself reached a peak of 108 in 1853. Thereafter the number began to decline and Manchester was surpassed as the largest centre of cotton spinning by Bolton in the 1850s and Oldham in the 1860s. However, this period of decline coincided with the rise of the city as the financial centre of the region.

Manchester continued to process cotton, and in 1913, 65% of the world's cotton was processed in the area.

The First World War interrupted access to the export markets. Cotton processing in other parts of the world increased, often on machines produced in Manchester. Manchester suffered greatly from the Great Depression and the underlying structural changes that began to supplant the old industries, including textile manufacture.

THE BLITZ.

Like most of the UK, the Manchester area was mobilised extensively during the Second World War. For example, casting and machining expertise at Beyer peacock and company's locomotive works in Gorton was switched to bomb-making; Dunlop's rubber works in Chorlton-on-Medlock made barrage balloons; and just outside the city in Trafford Park, engineers Metropolitan-Vickers made Avro Manchester & Avro Lancaster bombers & Ford built the Rolls-Royce Merlin engines to power them. Manchester was thus the target of bombing by the Luftwaffe, and by late 1940 air raids were taking place against non-military targets.

The biggest took place during the "Christmas Blitz" on the nights of 22/23 and 24 December 1940, when an estimated 474 tonnes (467 long tons) of high explosives plus over 37,000 incendiary bombs were dropped.

A large part of the historic city centre was destroyed, including 165 warehouses, over 200 + business premises,

& 150 offices. 376 Mancunian civilians were killed and more than 30,000 houses were damaged. Manchester Cathedral,

Royal Exchange and Free Trade Hall were among the buildings seriously damaged; restoration of the cathedral took 20 years.

POST SECOND WORLD WAR.

Cotton processing and trading continued to fall in peacetime, and the exchange closed in 1968. By 1963 the port of Manchester was the UK's third-largest and employed over 3,000 men, but the canal was unable to handle the increasingly large container ships. Traffic declined, and the port closed in 1982. The heavy industry suffered a downturn from the 1960s and was greatly reduced under the economic policies followed by Margaret Thatcher's government after 1979. Manchester lost 150,000 jobs in manufacturing between 1961 and 1983.

Regeneration began in the late 1980s, with initiatives such as the Metrolink, the Bridgewater concert hall, the Manchester Arena, and (in Salford) the rebranding of the port as Salford Quays. Two bids to host the Olympic Games were part of a process to raise the international profile of the city.

Manchester has a history of attacks attributed to Irish Republicans, including Manchester's martyrs of 1867, arson in 1920, a series of explosions in 1939, and two bombs in 1992. On Saturday 15 June 1996, the Provisional Irish Republican Army is known as the (IRA) carried out the 1996 Manchester bombing, the detonation of a large bomb next to a department store in the city centre. The largest to be detonated on British soil, the bomb injured over 200 people, heavily damaged nearby buildings, and broke windows 1/2 mile (800 m) away. The cost of the immediate damage was initially estimated at £50 million, but this was quickly revised upwards. The final insurance payout was over £400 million; many affected businesses never recovered from the loss of trade.

SINCE THE 2000S (MILLENNIUM)

Spurred by the investment after the 1996 bomb and aided by the XVII Commonwealth games the city centre has undergone extensive regeneration.

New and improved renovated complexes such as The Printworks and Corn exchange have become popular shopping, eating and entertainment areas. Manchester Arndale is the UK's largest city-centre shopping centre.

Large city sections from the 1960s have been demolished, re-developed or modernised with the use of glass and steel. Old mills have been converted into apartments. Hulme has undergone extensive regeneration, with million-pound loft-house apartments being developed. The 47-storey, 554-foot

(169 m) Beetham tower was the tallest UK building outside London and the highest residential accommodation
in Europe when completed in 2006. It was surpassed in
2018 by the 659-foot (201 m) South Tower of the Deansgate
square project, also in Manchester. In January 2007, the
independent Casino Advisory Panel licensed Manchester
to build the UK's only super casino, but plans were abandoned in February 2008.

On 22 May 2017, when Islamic extremist (Salman
Ramadan Abedi) carried out a bombing at an Ariana
Grande concert in the Manchester arena; the bomb killed
23, including himself and injured over 800 civilians. It
was the deadliest terrorist attack and the first suicide
bombing in Britain since the 7 July 2005 London bomb-
ings, relevant to this part of the chapter is because later
on through the years as I travelled through the prison
system I ended up in the high-security jail of (HMP
FRANKLAND) up north near Newcastle.

I met Omar one of the bombers that failed to detonate
his bomb on the train and I asked him (why) he started
getting all political about opinions and the government
so I left him to it but I thought it was crazy the way his
mind worked & how he could strap a bomb to himself
or furthermore try detonate homemade explosives in a
public place it's beyond the normal human thought.

But as a human of understanding and seeing other
peoples views I understood where he was coming from to

a certain extent because he felt England & the Americans due to the war was killing and raping his people back home, Omar got 35 years + so I don't think he will ever get released from the concrete grave but my prayers are with him and those that lost their lives.

Around the world, though it caused worldwide condemnation and changed the UK's threat level to "critical" for the first time since 2007.

Since around the turn of the 21st century, Manchester has been regarded as one of the candidates for the unofficial title of the second city of the United Kingdom alongside Birmingham by sections of the international press, British public, and government ministers.

Manchester and Birmingham traditionally compete as front runners for this unofficial title.

SPORTING TOWN.

Manchester is well known as a city of sport. Two decorated Premier League football clubs bear the city name – Manchester United & Manchester City. Manchester United play its home games at Old Trafford, in the Manchester suburb of Trafford, the largest club football ground in the United Kingdom. Manchester City's home ground is the City of Manchester stadium (also known as the Etihad Stadium for sponsorship purposes); its former ground, Maine Road was demolished in 2003.

The City of Manchester Stadium was initially built as the main athletics stadium for the 2002 commonwealth games and was then reconfigured into a football stadium before Manchester City's arrival. Manchester has hosted domestic, continental and international football competitions at Fallowfield Stadium, Maine Road, Old Trafford, & the City of Manchester stadium. Competitions hosted in the city include the FIFA World Cup (1996), UEFA European Championships (1996), Olympic football (2012), UEFA Champion League Final (2003), UEFA Cup Final (2008), four FA Cup finals (1893, 1911, 1915, 1970) and three League cup finals (1977, 1978, 1984).

First-class sporting facilities were built for the 2002 commonwealth games including the City of Manchester Stadium, the National squash centre & the Manchester aquatic centre.

Manchester has competed twice to host the Olympic Games, beaten by Atlanta for 1996 and Sydney for 2000. The National cycling centre includes a velodrome, BMX Arena and Mountainbike trials, and is the home of the British Cycling team, UCI ProTeam Team Sky and Sky Track Cycling.

The Manchester Velodrome was built as a part of the bid for the 2000 games and has become a catalyst for British success in cycling.

The velodrome hosted the UCI Track Cycling world championships for a record third time in 2008. The

National Indoor BMX arena holds (2,000 capacity) adjacent to the velodrome opened in 2011. The Manchester Arena hosted the F.I.N.A World Swimming Championships in 2008. Manchester Cricket Club evolved into Lancashire County Cricket Club and play at Old Trafford cricket ground, as do Manchester originals, a new city-based cricket team founded in 2019 which will play in the new cricket competition.

(The Hundred) representing Lancashire and Manchester. Manchester also hosted the world squash championships in 2008, and also hosted the 2010 world lacrosse championships in July 2010.

Recent sporting events hosted by Manchester include the 2013 Ashes series, the 2013 Rugby league World Cup and the 2015 Rugby World Cup.

INTERNATIONAL RELATIONSHIPS.

Manchester has formal twinning arrangements or ("friendship agreements") with several places.

Besides, the British council maintains a metropolitan centre in Manchester.

Those places include the following.

Netherlands, Nicaragua, Germany, Spain

Pakistan, USA, Rehovot, Israel

Saint Petersburg, Russia, Wuhan the People's Republic of China & Australia.

Manchester is home to the largest group of consuls in the UK outside London.

The expansion of international trade links during the Industrial Revolution led to the introduction of the first consuls in the 1820s and since then over 800, from all parts of the world, have been based in Manchester. Manchester hosts consular services for most of the north of England.

PROUD MANCUNIAN.

I have to say I am very proud to be from Manchester and to be a Mancunian.

Born and raised from the days growing up as a kid there was no place like it and it's considered to be one of the best places in the world to live. Well, I could not agree more despite the dark clouds which seem to hover over the Mancunian people due to the weather being so miserable it's a beautiful place and I'm sure many are proud to be Mancunian just like me.

I love my home town and before I start with my book I thought I'd give the readers across the world access to the knowledge of my beloved home town of MANCHESTER and the history we have plus how we opened many doors for traders to live and earn a decent wage the Mancunian people stuck together as you can see throughout history.

Much love to my Mancunian people and the rest of the world I hope you enjoy the rest of my book and I hope it brings you knowledge and wisdom, especially if kids & teenagers are reading this even though I don't discriminate against age or colour this is for everybody.

Like I said previously my book is intended to tell my story but at the same time give knowledge of life and how we can make changes but also have faith for things to change, because I know there's a lot of brothers & sisters out there in the world that need assistance so if I can open up certain minds with food for thought which is my intention then I'm happy.

Even if I only touch one out of a thousand people I've done my work but it don't stop there because the struggle continuously continues and we stay fighting as long as you got a heartbeat and air to breathe you can make it happen. Blessings upon blessings may everyone live in love peace & harmony without the hate.

FROM MANCHESTER WITH LOVE.

CHAPTER TWO

Welcome, 2 My World.
What I Remember.

My name is Aaron Nathan Grossman aka LOCZDA6IXTH born on the sixth day of the sixth month of 1987.

Born at St Mary's hospital Rusholme, Manchester.

Not sure of the time or not like it's any more important than my government name being what is on paper so I can't say I am that fussed about knowing the times of my birth because it doesn't hold any significant importance to me or neither shall it for the reader so that's why I haven't gained the knowledge of that particular part of my life history.

I commence and start with my thoughts emotions and feelings on the first stages of our human life, in my opinion, the beginning of everyone's life is nothing but one big ball of excitement mixed with curiosity especially as we're growing to discover the world as we see it through the eyes of children and having our little personalities which is what makes us all unique as human beings.

The mechanisms within our brains don't function that well for you to understand what's going on around you in too much detail plus in my opinion, we even struggle to know either right from wrong therefore as Children we should not be deemed as "troublesome" or "outcasted" but rather looked at as (misguided) but most definitely misunderstood, but growing up seeing what you wasn't suppose to see as a child could affect the way you see and view things so understanding a person before we judge them would prevent the (misunderstanding) an also the wrong perception of that human being.

As far back as I can remember as a young mixed-race boy I never thought or dreamed my life would become what it has today better yet go through all the trials and tribulations that I've fought along the journey of my life, but unfortunately, that's due to certain circumstances that I had no control over being a child so I take that with a pinch of salt and will explain throughout the biography the why's the how's also my thought process growing up with very little support from my dad and my mum being a single parent.

Through the eyes of mine, I take my hat off to my mum because she weathered the storm held it down for me and my sister had various jobs but most times she held down a couple of cleaning jobs and worked at many other places too to support us, she wasn't shy about working a low-income occupation that only pays people around the average of £3.60+ which was calculated at the legal minimum wages back in the early 1990s so it wasn't just my mum in that position coming from a deprived area a lot off single mothers was dependent on social income-related paychecks even milk tokens were issued to the people at the low end of the spectrum.

Even though my mum did work from time to time with part-time jobs maybe her circumstances would off been a bit different having a full-time occupation because of the expenses that were coming out due to bills and stuff it was hard plus depending on overtime at work which I don't think she could do that much because she had responsibilities as a mother plus she had no money for babysitters she needed all the money she could save and there was no help or assistance from my dad so she had to do what she had to do not only for herself but for me and my sister.

Despite my mums' income level of money being as hard as it was for her plus without the assistance from my absent dad I can say my mum always found a way to provide so we never went without food or clothes presents at Christmas birthdays etc, but sporting the latest fabrics or the latest trainers at a young age didn't have any relevance to me I didn't have a clue what designer names were so my mum could off put me in anything I didn't give a shit about it let alone know about and care for designer name's that meant nothing to me nor would I be the one that wanted to stand out, I was more observant not shy but I was a quiet one so being loud never really appealed to me but on the other hand the only thing what I thought I was missing still hadn't had no relevance to me at the time which was my fathers presence because when I think back it's like I never knew him or worse that he never even "existed" it was just my mum raising me single handed with no father figure standing beside her, even the thought of having a dad didn't cross my mind because like I said previous to this I had no relationship with him therefore he wasn't in my thoughts at that stage of my young life (period) which is quite sad for a young man but it was just me and my sister Natalie back than who is three years older than me even Natalie's dad josh at the time wasn't around so not only having mine or my sisters dad absent there was absolutely no man apart from my mums cousins, I wasn't even thought about when my mum was with Josh I was still in my dads nuts so that relationship they had was years before which obviously came to an end for reasons I'm unable to disclose due to having unknown knowledge of that relationship or breakup.

(Let the past, be the past).

Because sometimes some things are just better left unknown and better left unsaid. (Keep it pushing).

Thinking back on memories of my dad coming to visit me at my home are very blurry like I'm underwater without wearing goggles so I can just about see through the cloudy visits he used to do which weren't very often so between (1987) and (1994) the relationship with my dad was nothing other than flying visitation where he would pull up in his white Nissan bluebird taxi that he used to drive because working for a taxi service was his occupation back then in early 1990, he only ever spent a considerable amount of time before leaving so I guess those pit stops affected the way I saw him as a dad because it was just now and then he would make an appearance, but even those appearances weren't memorable for me that much because we have never done anything together or anything actively active with each other so that's another downside of the way our relationship turned out.

In the mix off growing up in all what seemed to be just normal living for me and my sister we had no physical or mental-emotional problems so life was good and we enjoyed it despite having no fathers because we had quite a big family unit so it was never a dull moment for fun because it's not like we didn't have another family an close friends to play with we had younger cousins two girls which my mums' sister Alice had to her other half at the time called Clinton which were named Rachel and Jacqueline Grossman, we were all close with each other the relationship we shared as well as the bond we had was warming it was just like that with many of our other relatives the family tree on my mums' side was very very well connected strong.

My mum also has a first cousin called Caroline but I grew up calling her aunty Caz coz it sounded better she had no children but she used to look after me and my sister like we were her own she cared for us a great deal and lived with us for a little while with her boyfriend warren who was from Ireland but he used to stay and live here in England so he'd come and stay a few times a week but I remember him having his own flat that he used to rent just down the road from where I lived on (Birchlane) because I think he wanted to be close not only for his work but also to be close to my auntie Caroline.

I looked up to Warren he was a good guy in my eyes like an older brother or uncle type used to treat me and my sister good take us to the shops and buy us sweets pick us up take us out in his flashy cars he always loved to speed thinking back I suppose he was a bit of a speed (junky) so my sister never really wanted to come plus my auntie Caroline used to go mad at him for speeding with us but I used to love it and he could see that due to the big smile on my little face, I wasn't scared.

My other auntie (Julie Everall) was my mum's right hand growing up who also had children to her other half at the time called Keith Wilks.

Filtering through just a few names of the Wilks family are Manuel, Geni, Marcus, Raya, Levi, their grandma Ethline Wilks AkA (ETTY) (REST IN PEACE) sadly passed away she was a very strong and good-hearted woman the foundation of the Wilks family their family tree stretches far and beyond also related to the Thompson's, there are so many people to bless it's just nearly impossible for me to mention everybody's name but my love and blessings continue to grow for everyone nobody here left out.

Julie's kids were all girls and the bond we had and shared was unbreakable, to say the least, they were older than me by a handful of years so they had those older sister characteristics about them even though I already had an older sister Natalie they were there religiously that's how you know there love was real authentic an without a doubt I can say Naomi Leah and Tyrah kept me and Natalie from harm's way and we all grew up with the same energy despite living separately or going to different schools we were tight like some perfectly knitted fresh garments.

Many other relatives such as nephews, nieces, and cousins are hanging off my Irish family tree so there's many I've never met and don't know off that well with most of them always living in Ireland.

Lily & Eamonn Carolines mum & dad, my great grandmother Annie Lilys sister my mums mum Margaret Mary marjoram, Debra, Lisa, Ryan, Sharon, Lauren, Morgon Caroline's brother, Tracy, Jason, Harriet Margaret Morgans mother was Eamonn's sister so Reece Kady Keeley is the children of Margaret plus her eldest son Christian stokes not quite up to date with the history of their father but even I can't remember ever seeing him around when I was growing up with my cousins.

Reece kady Keeley and Christian also have kids so it does get deep but how deep is the rabbit hole as they say and it's how deep you are willing to go to discover your family ancestry.

Most of the family from both sides will be in the second chapter family as I explain my blood history from top to bottom.

Margaret Morgan was unforgettable as she is unfortunately passed away due to ill health and that's when as a kid I remember my mum dressing me and my sister up in the smartest off clothes with my little bow tie and a neatly shaven head with the patterns init. I remember being intrigued and asking my mum what's the occasion because I didn't understand what was happening or have any understanding of death or funerals.

I was sat in the church looking into my mother's eyes thinking why you got water falling from your eyes it was like it was a spiritual frequency that just locked as I thought what I was thinking she looked at me wiping away the tears with a light smile leaned in with both arms gave me a big squeeze and told me everything is fine and she'll be ok.

So that's the first time I was too ever go to my first funeral where everything just felt so dark like there was a dark cloud hovering over everything It's a chapter in my life that I remember bright as a day not only because it was a sad moment for the family but she had a wonderful loving character and was loved by many which resulted in her having a beautiful send off she'll forever be missed and loved. (R.I.P) (Margaret Morgan).

Being surrounded by mostly girls in my family growing up I only had a few male older relatives so I can't forget my older cousins Reece and my wrestling partner Ryan we had many play fights which sometimes ended badly for both of us in all sorts of ways and I mean hospitalised having to have stitches in different body parts we were a crazy bunch of wild fearless kids with no fear.

His older sister Lisa was my sisters' partner too as they had the same likes in music clothes and the energy they shared was good the family tree list goes way back as I can remember and I can't exactly remember to put everybody's name in because some aren't here with us no more whether they rest in peace peacefully so I apologise to all long lost family if I fail to mention you but my love will always be written in indelible ink use are forever in my heart may are spiritual frequencies forever be locked together.

Back to what I remember with the history and relationship between me and my dad is little more than just being someone's son whereas, in reality, you would think it's a bond that you would share with your offspring forever with the love and happiness plus guidance you would give despite not being together with the mother of your children.

Regardless of whether they're divorced/separated or simply just live apart for whatever reasons they may be at the time but In my case as well as probably many other kids around the world that wasn't how it turned it out to be so as we get older we learn how to deal with emotions that may cause us to react in certain ways especially when it's family because ("those close to you hurt you the most") but the one thing (you can choose your friends but you can't choose your family) which I was always told by my mum.

The main issue I had to deal with growing up was not knowing who my siblings were because I vaguely remember my mum mentioning I had older brothers from my dads' side which I never knew about so for me it was intriguing to know and to find out who these people were as I think any young man too found out he had bigger brothers or other family members you didn't know it would make any young boy think and be happy that he's got older siblings especially bigger brothers. Unfortunately, we never had that brotherly love and bond between us and that's all the doings of the selfishness of my dads' betrayal and disloyalty he had for the offspring that he created.

So for years and years, I grew up not knowing who other parts of my family tree on my dad's side we're until I got older and was able to ask questions for myself and do my homework on discovering who people were for myself and to draw the dots to connect the relationship between everyone.

On the other hand, the relationship between me and my dads' side of the family was a bit strange, to say the least, whether or not it was a negative reaction due to emotions carried by people who didn't know me or whether it was me being paranoid not knowing these people who are supposed to be my family but all I can remember to thinking was positive thoughts like I'm just your blood related relative meaning my dad was part of me so I'm interested in getting to know but unfortunately for me, the welcoming I received was somewhat a bit confusing for me and I felt I wasn't part off that side of the family, it was a weird feeling but I guess it's just part of the emotions we carry when we enter something new that we ain't familiar with.

The only reason I say that is because I can remember on many occasions going to my grandma's house who lived in Longsight Manchester and the few visits that I made there the greeting that I received felt a bit cold especially from my dads' sister Sheila or Janet I'm not sure which one-off them it was but she'd open the door see me stood there sometimes it would be raining and I would off travelled a few miles on my bike and the response I would get after me asking her if my nana was home ("Noshes at the shops or the market call back tomorrow or I'll tell her you called") before I get a chance to respond "I hear those words which I think should never come from a family members mouth (which are) ("what is your name") I stand there with a kind of shocked look on my face with how she didn't know who I was and I'm looking at her thinking I'm your brother's son also it's raining and your not going to offer me in out the cold, I'd respond with my names Aaron I'm (Dougles) son (aka) (Preacher) the look on her face would be a smile an and (OK) short sweet and very awkward for me at that time and it did kind off make me feel disconnected because I did feel outcasted and when she asked who I was it made me feel unknown to that side of the family so that's why I said previously in this chapter about my dads' selfishness and how his disloyalties kept me disconnected also distant from all an probably most off the family tree on my dads' side and don't hold any grudges for that because it's not in any way either of my aunties faults for feeling how they did its life and it's all about accepting how things are sometimes and dealing with emotions.

The welcoming I used to get before I was welcomed properly into the family home of my Grandmas house was none other than the way the dynamics were due to my dad breaking that bond which I should off had with all of my dads' brothers and sisters, nieces nephews cousins even my brothers which I had were older junior and Nicolas who I never knew or grew up around didn't know Nicolas but knew off junior because his mum Linda was friends with my mum and due to my dad having junior they had some sort of understanding motherly relationship but In all honesty, I think they were just friends.

Thinking back on what I remembered off how it was, I don't blame or have any negative feelings whatsoever towards my aunties and Uncles being how it was because I can't say I had a bad connection with all of the relatives from my dads' side because I had a genuinely real relationship with them once I started going, my second cousins Natalie and her little brother Miguel had a good relationship and we got on well together so when I did get to go my grandma's house we did play games, computer and as young men, we used to toy fight a lot an act out the moves on each other from the street fighter or mortal combat and most definitely wrestling (WWF) was the wave back then just like how I explained with me and my other cousin (Ryan) but my Grandma was old school very strict and didn't like us fighting because we would be making a racket so all the banging and noises were noticed then we would hear her shouting from the bottom of the stairs (Oi you 2 stop all the De noise chuh) in her Jamaican accent. (R.I.P) my grandma Daphne long live your soul.

I'm not going to go into too much detail or try to remember half of what I seem to understand to remember as a child as this is just the beginning of when my windows first opened to the world so I'm sharing my thought process also giving an insight into the mind frame of a child of how I see and saw things growing up or the way how life can shape your future from what you see also exposed too.

So if you ain't strong enough to overcome certain obstacles within the mind you will struggle not that it's going to be easy to do because obviously, it's going to be difficult but most importantly it's learning how to accept maybe your own mistakes and faults or controlling those emotions from past bad experiences for whatever reason that maybe we all have the ability within it just takes something to click before we start to make those changes because they say you can't change yourself until you change your surroundings.

Many people succumb to the pressures of life and if we're not careful those pipes can burst and lead to many different negative forces entering your life it's easier said than done when it comes to eradicating the negativity your energy can decrease especially when you think you are in a hole too deep for you get out from.

But sometimes it's that hole that you find yourself in that makes you rebuild from the start and rethink also evaluate what's most valuable and important in your life.

Plus it's hard sometimes not to think about certain past choices whether we were kids seeing things we shouldn't have seen we can't un-see things our eyes see so we have to keep it pushing keep striving regret can fester. Regret for inaction or paths not taken do not go away as easily. These linger and fester in our brains.

While we can actively cope with poorly chosen actions we've taken, options foregone lead us to wonder incessantly about what might've happened.

THROUGH THE EYES OF MINE.

CHAPTER THREE

The Tree of Life.
(Bloods Thicker Than Water).

Before I start the process of this chapter I'd like to share my thoughts on family life. That I believe it's defined as the routine interactions and activities that a family have together. When members of a family enjoy each other's company and spend a lot of time doing things together, sharing the love & experiences that's my definition and example of a good strong happy family life.

Most importantly and what you always have to remember is that Family is the single most important influence in a child's life. From their first moments of life, children depend on parents and family to protect them and provide for their needs. Parents and family form a child's first relationships. Family provides all members with security, identity and values, regardless of age there should not be any form of discrimination or differentiation.

Welcome to my family:

"In 1629 a large group of Irish men and women were sent to Guiana, and by 1632, Irish were the main slaves sold to Antigua and Montserrat in the West Indies.

By 1637 a census showed that 69% of the total population of Montserrat were Irish slaves, which records show was a cause of concern to the English planters."

The original inhabitants of Jamaicans are believed to be the Arawaks, also called Tainos. They came from South America 2,500 years ago and named the island Xaymaca, which meant "land of wood and water". The Arawaks were a mild and simple people by nature.

Gaining the knowledge of my black and white ancestors helps me get a sense of direction not only to give you as the reader information and knowledge on the historical history of how the Irish and Jamaicans share a similar way of being treated regardless of their colour because not many people know that 69% of the people living in Montserrat were Irish slaves which I will explain in detail, and for those that are thinking what's this got to do with my family tree, well my answer is simply (ABSOLUTELY NOTHING) but in some ways, it's too help also assist those coming from Irish and Jamaican descent like me get a better understanding.

I'll try not to take up too much of your time speaking about the history of my descent but I've spent so much time seeking this information involving the inherited inheritance of both of these countries as part of my culture, therefore, it's only right for those that share the same similar bloodline I think it's very important to gain the knowledge to be aware of how our ancestors shaped our world before our time also the things that we may never get told because we may be from a place but not really from that place because history has shown from the knowledge I've required which is there for everyone too research has been hidden for centuries, plus that there was an influx of people being sent from pillar to post as immigrated immigrants and being forced to change there whole life and personalities and even down to there language.

Irish immigration to Jamaica occurred primarily through the importation of Irish prisoners of war and indentured servants after the Irish rebellion of 1641 and also constituted the second-largest recorded ethnic influx into the country.

The first wave of Irish immigrants occurred in the early 17th century, Irish emigrant principally sailors, servants, and merchants. Many of the poorer emigrants were displaced Gaelic-Irish and Anglo-Irish Catholics, as well as convicts who were indentured servants. Many of the indentured servants were transported unwillingly. More than 2,000 children alone were sent on ships from Galway Bay.

Of those surviving the long journey many more succumbed to disease, the harsh conditions and unfamiliar tropical conditions.

One of the first English colonies in the Caribbean was established in Barbados in 1626. Irish merchant families from towns like Galway Kinsale and Waterford established their trading networks in the Caribbean.

In terms of citizenship, all Jamaicans who moved to the UK before Jamaican Independence in 1962 were automatically granted British citizenship because Jamaica was an overseas colony of the country. Jamaican immigrants must now apply for citizenship if they wish to become British nationals. It refers to the ship MV Empire Windrush, which docked in Tilbury on 22 June 1948, bringing workers from Jamaica, Trinidad and Tobago and other islands, to help fill post-war UK labour shortages. The ship carried 492 passengers - many of them children.

But also many of the immigrated immigrants were not only transferred for labour a lot of these later arrivals came from Jamaica's capital and largest city, Kingston where the divide between rich and poor is much more evident than other places on the island. Most first-generation immigrants moved to Britain to seek an improved standard of living, escape violence or find employment. By 1956, more than 40,000 immigrants from the West Indies had moved to Britain. New immigration rules were introduced in the intervening years before the Immigration Act 1971 changed the law to grant only temporary residence to most people arriving from Commonwealth countries. The people known as immigrants from the Windrush era off 1948 to between early 1970,s It has been confirmed that: anyone from the 'Windrush' generation can become a British citizen. the free citizenship offer will apply not just to the families of Caribbean migrants who came to the UK between 1948 and 1973 but to anyone from other Commonwealth nations who settled in the UK over the same period. But Some were treated as illegal immigrants. Some lost jobs, homes, benefits and access to the NHS. ... To amplify this insult, legal citizens were placed in immigration detention centres and some deported. Those abroad on holiday were refused back into the only country they had ever known.

Discovering the knowledge of how the colonial government was back in the 16th and 17th centuries is an indication of my life today and how it is shaped due to where I was born and bred because my Caribbean side of the family is from Portland known as a parish on the northeast coast of the island of Jamaica.

Port Antonio is the small, laid-back capital, with faded colonial-era mansions lining the Titchfield Peninsula.

Sandy beaches fringe the forested coast between the city and the deep waters of the Blue Lagoon farther east. Inland, bamboo rafts ply the Rio Grande river. Trails cross the Blue Mountains, known for their coffee plantations. The Rio Grande is a river of Jamaica, found in the parish of Portland. It was named after Spanish occupied Jamaica in the 15th and 16th centuries. One of the largest rivers in Jamaica, it was named "Big River" by the Spanish. It is one of the many tourist attractions in Portland and is used mainly for rafting, also The Guava River rises just north of the Grand Ridge of the Blue Mountains on the border of Portland Parish in Jamaica. From here it runs east then north and then east again to its confluence with the Rio Grande. In this land off clear waters and beautiful beaches, that's also surrounded by the culture of the colonial Jamaican people is where my dad's dad Frank Cargill my grandfather was born in 1935.

Portland Jamaica is where my grandmother Daphne Lewis lived and was born and raised and only came to England in the 1960s before the British laws changed for overseas none English people to require British citizenship this helped her and many others at the time as Jamaica was part of the British colony so it gave the Jamaican people access to the UK, but like I mentioned before in this article that Jamaican immigrants that were taken unwillingly from Jamaica and brought to England were refused entry back into England when they went back to visit family in Jamaica and most of them being children England was the only place they've ever known.

I'm kind of blessed to realise that my great ancestry's bloodline whether that be from my mother's side in Ireland or my dad's side in Jamaica because gaining the knowledge and knowing that even though many of the people weren't related to me it's still sad to know that many people didn't make it due to ill health and poor living conditions in the wind rush era off 1948. It's kind of interesting and intriguing how my families historical history has become divided into two different generations being one white and one black because back in the early 1960s especially in England it was hard for a black man to live let alone have a white woman as his girlfriend plus it was difficult for white women to be with black men England was deemed an ignorant place, it's a shame that things were the way they were due too many of the people who gave their blood sweat and tears to rebuild England and was from the tropics of the tropical islands like Jamaica and many other tropical colonial countries so in my opinion human beings shouldn't off been treated differently from being a different colour but that's another story due to racism/discriminatory factors it's diabolical that this shit still happens today and it's not even behind closed doors either.

When my dad's father Frank Cargill came to England in 1956, he moved to London where he worked and resigned until his retirement between 1982-1983 then flew back to his homeland off Portland Jamaica but sadly passed away in 1998 but was blessed to be able to live out the rest off his days in his homeland of the parish of beautiful Portland Jamaica.

For thirty years that he did stay here in England he worked at the Mcvities biscuit factory for nearly almost the whole off the 30 year's in London he never lived in Manchester where my dad eventually came due to his mum living in Manchester when she finally arrived from Portland Jamaica in the 1960s.

Whilst daphne my grandmother was settling in England her occupation for almost 40 years was working with the N.H.S and with their dad already working in England Capital my dad and Sheila my dads younger sister was still living back in Portland Jamaica with their grandmother Rebecca daphne's mum until they came to England in early 1970,s if I'm correct around 1974.

Living with mum daphne coming from Jamaica adapting to the way of English life as I said previously it was different and a lot of the English people were ignorant to the fact that black people were in their country taking their jobs getting their women pregnant and having mix raced babies also complaining there getting free help assistance from the N.H.S.

Sheila born in 1959 is 3 years younger than her brother my dad Dougal who was born in 1956 both are second names taken after the there-fathers name which is Cargill.

With both still finding their feet being in England living with their mum money was needed not only just for food and rent but many other reasons such as living, because the money they had was tight back then so being eighteen and getting off his arse, was the thing to do so my dads occupation at the time was working in various factories but once held down an occupation working for a taxi company meanwhile Sheila was studying to become a social worker working towards her goal applying for apprenticeships in the field of child care. As the time went by moving on forward a few years finally adapting to the new way of life living in England Manchester with his mum and sister Sheila daphne fell pregnant in the early 1960s to her other half at the time called Ossie Richards and eventually would give birth to another three beautiful children named Micheal Janet and Leon. They all grew up in the same household together in Longsight Manchester and had a good close bond plus their connection was good and with my dad being the eldest he took on a bit of the responsibility as well as Sheila giving his mum assistance where it was needed.

I'm unaware of the in-depth details of Ossie's life so I'm afraid there's no information whatsoever I can give the reader nor myself other than what I'm giving you there's nothing on the way his and my grandmother's relationship was apart from the conversations I've had with my uncles and aunts so I can't give you anything else other than the information I've received and what I already know but I was told Ossie was a good man humble was family orientated quiet had his bad days just like everybody else but a pleasant man. My nana Daphne Lewis like I said previously was a good woman some times hard also strict but a wonderfully positive woman all-around caring and most importantly loved her family. The three children which I mentioned what my grandmother Daphne had when she came to England in the 1960's after leaving Jamaica were all raised in Britain. I'm not too sure what Michael's occupation was when he was growing up but I know he was into his music and the creative side of music production and working with different programs but unfortunately fell ill for a good few year's due to the stresses off work but after overcoming some hard times he eventually found his mojo again and got his mind healthier still a little fragile to this day but he's back on track an most importantly better and stronger than ever before he also had two children named Natalie and her little brother Miguel part off the Richards family.

My auntie Janet on the other hand if I can recall worked a few different jobs but worked at the jobcentre not sure which department but I know it was for a considerable period my auntie Sheila like I explained previously, was in the profession working with children I think like foster care looking after kids who've had a difficult upbringing due to bad things happening in their life or having no parents or family.

My dad again going back was in between different jobs like working in factories, doing security work and also was a taxi driver for a considerable amount of years. Last but not least before I continue I would like to take the time out to give my love and utmost respect to my uncle (LEON RICHARDS) who sadly passed away in the year 2019.

Leon was a good man and was a wizard on computers also worked as an I.T technical consultant for the banks and very much was into his health and fitness and the way he lived his life was a strict code of living he never smoked and If I can recall never was a big drinker either bit off a fitness fanatic so it's amazingly unfair and unfortunate that he was taken away from us so early leaving behind a good life with his family and a beautiful daughter my niece (Jolie Richards Clayton) it's a Shame too when he was only in his early 50,s especially with the athletic build and athleticism he had just never would off thought that the Lord had other plans for him so I send my love through words and wisdom and may the angels protect his spirit and may his soul rest in internal peace Leon you will forever be missed and most definitely always remembered within our hearts. We love you dearly.

After arriving in England in the early 1970s being here for almost over a decade is when my dad (Dougle Cargill) met my mother Margaret Mary Marjoram they had me in the summer of June 1987 and then 7 years later, again my mum fell pregnant in 1994 and gave birth to another little boy at ST MARYS hospital Rusholme Manchester who she named Rumal Jake Grossman.

My dad would eventually go on to have six boys one girl all but I and Rumal have different mothers so I'm not aware of the history between him and the other women but as I explained in the first chapter

(WHAT I REMEMBER) it's all part of the lost connection we had growing up separately, my brother's names are eldest to youngest (JUNIOR) (RUMAL) (TREY) and (LEON).

My younger sister is a distant memory for me because I have no clue who she is or where she is all I know is what I was told of my dad from asking questions is that the mother who he had the child to was unwell and ended up being sectioned with mental health issues, therefore, she was unable to be considered fit to look after the child.

I don't know the reasons behind her illness or why she fell ill I don't even know her government name I'm even unable to disclose even my little sister's name because I believe she was taken away from birth by social services and placed into the hands of strangers to be raised and looked after and because my dad was absent from the birth date for reasons I don't know the hospital had no details or any information on who the father was at the time due to their break-up a few months before she gave birth but the good thing that's come out of this bad situation is that my auntie Sheila being connected in that field and has been for many years has been trying to discover the whereabouts of my little sister an the last time I received any information is that she was being fostered by a family somewhere in England but unfortunately my hopes off finding her have come to a dead end so my prayers go out to my lost sister an if you ever get to read this book one day just know you've found me it will be a blessing that one day we finally get to be reunited as brother and sister I'll forever have faith not doubt. I love you.

Special shout-out goes to my little brother (Trey Wilson) who unfortunately got convicted of murder and was handed a life sentence at the age of nineteen and has to serve a minimum of 19 years in custody before eligible for parole.

My prayers are vows that you make it out healthy become free & stay free and that I hope you find the process of reintegration back into society blessed & stress-free.

There's a lot of cousins and nephews also nieces aunties uncles to mention on my dad's side with brothers having kids of their own to women I don't know so even though they're my distant family it's difficult for me to mention everyone who I ain't already mentioned especially with having more family over in Portland Jamaica. Because that's where it all began for my Caribbean people here in England.

As far as I'm aware from what I was told and from also gaining my knowledge of the Caribbean bloodline off my historical history within the structure of my West Indies family is only one half off my family tree. We now move onto my Irish side and where it all began for my mother's mother Margaret Mary Marjoram before she came to England in the early (1950's).

Drimnagh (Droimneach) is a suburb of Dublin, Ireland, situated on the Southside of the city between Walkinstown, Crumlin and Inchicore bordered by the grand canal the north and east. Drimnagh is in the postal district Dublin 12. Drimnagh derives its name from the word drum each, or country with ridges. ... The lands of Drimnagh were taken from their Irish owners by Strongbow, who gave them to the Barnwell family, who had arrived in Ireland with Strongbow in 1167 and had settled in Berehaven in Munster. With a population of around 12,000, Drimnagh is a massive community with plenty of young families, along with long-time residents.

By the 9th century, there was an Anglo-Saxon settlement here.

In the Middle Ages, improved drainage methods led to population growth. In the late Victorian and Edwardian periods, its rural character made it popular among the middle-class. The loss of its railway station, the conversion of larger houses into flats or bedsitters, and significant social housing development to the south of the area changed its character again in the 1970s.

Historically, Chorlton was a village on Lancashire's southern border with Cheshire and a township within the ancient parish of Manchester. It was incorporated into the city of Manchester in 1904. Chorlton borders Stretford, Sale, Didsbury, Withington, and Whalley range. The River Mersey runs past Chorlton along its southern boundary. The area's eastern boundary has changed since the 19th century because of incorporation into the City of Manchester and division into wards. Irish immigrants came to work in the expanding industries of Manchester, in small-scale horticulture and farming and domestic services.

They brought Roman Catholicism, and by the first decade of the 20th century, a church (St Augustine's) and convent school had been established on High Lane. Several cinemas opened in the first half of the 20th century. The first was the Chorlton Pavilion bought by H. D. Moorhouse in 1909 followed by the Palais de Luxe in 1915. It closed in 1958. The Rivoli opened on Barlow Moor Road in 1936 and changed its name several times to the Essoldo, the Classic and the Shalimar before closing in the 1980s. Likewise, the Majestic on Manchester

Road had several names, the Savoy, the ABC and the Gaumont. There are no remaining cinemas in Chorlton with the nearest being in Manchester and other surrounding areas.

The Rivoli, before it became the Essoldo, the Classic and the Shalimar and finished as our last cinema this is where my mums mum Margaret Mary Marjoram worked for many years about a mile or so from where she lived so it was easy for her to travel not sure if she drove at the time but Cundiff road just off hardy Lane was just literally around the corner from the cinema that was situated on Barlow Moor Road Chorlton.

My mum's sister Alice was still living in Ireland with family so she arrived several years later while my mum was in England Chorlton with her mum and dad Bernard Grossman and Margaret Mary Marjoram. St. Joseph's Industrial Schools were established at 8 Richmond Grove, Victoria Park, Longsight, in 1871 to provide a Catholic education for the children of Catholics in the Victoria Park and Longsight area. St. Joseph's operated as an approved school from 1933 so it became more suitable for catholic children in the Manchester area to get a place because my mum grew up in the Chorlton and Medlock area which was a few miles out of her postal code.

Fast forwarding a good few years is when my auntie Alice came to England and settled with the rest of the family.

Due to their mum and dad having problems within their relationship it was the year between 1975-1976 when Bernard and Margaret Mary marjoram finally split up which then caused friction within the household and I don't think my grandmother Margaret was quite 100% in good health at the time either so she became more fragile plus it didn't help with Bernard being a heavy drinker every day he became more and more dependent on drink some would call it an say he was an alcoholic.

With my grandad assaulting my grandmother on daily basis one day she went to visit her sister Lily and that's when Lily noticed her black eyes and realised Bernard was hitting her sister so my uncles Tony and his brother Morgan took a trip to visit Bernard and battered him senseless nearly killing him and from that moment my grandmother never went back.

With the dynamics being a very volatile and difficult place to be within the household at that specific time not only for my mum but for her mum's health things didn't get any easier for the family household and her health dramatically deteriorated.

At the age of nine years old and with the dynamics rapidly changing plus my mum's education slightly disrupted my mum left England to go live back with family in Ireland with her mum's sister Annie.

My auntie Alice stayed in England and continued to go education and overcome the disruptive breakdown of her parent's relationship and gained the strength to power through some difficult situations.

Three to four years passed for my mum living in Ireland but when she first left with her bags in tow heading across the Irish sea she was only 9-10 years old so she didn't get to see her mum until she got the sad news that her mum had passed so she had to come back to England for the burial but then went to live with her mum's sister Lily in 1979. Caroline Lily's daughter who I class as my auntie because it suits her better and it's what my sister Natalie and I have always called her since knee-high but she is my mum's first cousin they grew up together tight for years done most things and shared alike too many things.

Ten or more years past and Caroline and my mum kind of grew up and went on to do their things not like they didn't see or be with each other it's just they got older and wanted to discover the world for themselves plus they had their personalities and was into different things. My mum is naturally quite and don't like confrontation and would rather avoid the drama or aggro she loves music and was more into reggae music than the standard stuff loved being around the Jamaican culture the food the people the party's the atmosphere she enjoyed it she felt relaxed because she told me that the Jamaican people welcomed her an made her feel at ease and comfortable.

Caroline was more of the opposite not loud but got a strong presence about her liked old Irish music more into the way of her own culture of life wasn't into the sort of atmosphere my mum was into because of the music but still was intrigued had a few songs from certain artists that she liked plus she had friends that were from the Caribbean islands her and my mum love the culture of the Jamaican people.

Caroline had a long time relationship with her other half called (ROBERT) after she split with Warren years after who was around me when I was younger who I mention a lot in my first chapter (WHAT I REMEMBER).

I didn't know at the time that Caroline was actually with Robert in the early 1980s and got back together a good few years after Warren left and went back to his homeland of Ireland.

Caroline met Warren a good few years before getting back with Robert I know it sounds confusing but it's reality.

Caroline and Warren met back in the early 1990s which is quite funny because she told me they met at the social office which is for the people who are at the low-income end of the spectrum in other words the (BENEFITS) centre which was also called receiving a (JIRO) money from the government.

He approached her and asked if she had some "rizla papers" "not considered romantic you'd think lol" which she didn't have but her friend Anne did.

She said they exchanged words met up a few times talked & walked got along felt the vibe plus they got on well, coz they were both Irish and I think he liked her even more because of that so they ended up being together for about 4 years.

Despite the breakup and the history Warren and my auntie Caroline shared she still had her first love with Robert so they reconnected with each other after she split with Warren.

Caroline loved and cared for Robert very much they were together decades and was in love with one another for around twenty plus years I could tell they shared a good solid bond the energy was good between them not to say they probably ain't had their fair share of bad days like all "relationships" but he was a good man very polite well mannered and didn't deserve to be taken from us especially from his kids and my auntie Caroline.

Unfortunately, Robert passed suffering from a brain tumour which the doctor only gave him 12 months to live after they found out but he was a fighter and lasted longer than expected.

I'm not quite sure how long that it is was before Robert passed but I know it broke my aunt's heart in a million pieces and it took many years for her to overcome the loss of her soul mate.

Special thanks go out to my auntie Caroline who is a strong woman as well hats off to her because she has had to overcome the loss of her husband Robert, and also fought breast cancer and I can't imagine or even try to compare the tragic news that you received that day.

I'm sure it would off probably destroy anyone's life and thought process I really can't comprehend the feeling.

Anyways you survived and came out the other side even a stronger woman and I just want to say may the higher spirits continue to heal you and I'm forever blessed that you fought and won the battle that soo many fall victim too and I just wish that your health continues to keep getting better stay winning because your a winner love you to death.

The late 1980s is when my mum met my dad Dougal Cargill if I'm correct around 1986 my sister Natalie was already here aged three years old before my mum fell pregnant with me in 1987.

Like I said previously at the start of chapter One (WHAT I REMEMBER) I grew up without my dad present so my mum and dad must have split practically before I was even born so it was just me and my sister Natalie. Seven years later was the year of 1994 when my mum fell pregnant again with my little brother Rumal Jake Grossman to my dad, I don't think they were together at the time officially maybe the relationship they had probably was hard for them to separate from each other especially if there were children involved as well the history they shared.

My auntie Alice had two children round about the same period as my mum to her other half Clinton they were named Jacqueline Grossman & Rachel Grossman.

The Grossman family is divided into sections Grossman being my mum's dads name Bernard Grossman who's parents was originally Jewish & English.

My mum's mother's name of Marjoram that being Irish also my auntie Carolines side of the Morgan/Payne family plus my auntie Julie with her daughters being from the Wilks family who's family are from Jamaica we are all connected in some way or another and there are many more siblings who I will mention as part of my family tree. My half brother junior on my dad's side has two girls and two boys Kyiren, Aaliyah, Jaysiejo, and Shilo.

My sister Natalie has two daughters Amara & Tyhea my son Azai Beresford Grossman.

My cousin Naomi has a boy & girl Omari & Shae, Leah has two daughters Elijah & Rumai, Tyrah has one daughter Ivayah, Manuel has 3 children Daraqai donaeo & destiny & Sorayah has her daughter named Anaiyah.

My other cousins from the Morgan side of the family spectrum have multiple siblings starting from the eldest being Christian with three children, Imani, Sienna, Ellias, Keeley has four children Ameishay, Versacè, Ravell & Tyce Rees has six children Tasia, Dante, Keiya, Elise, Lamei, Larees last but not least, of course, is Cady with two children Tia & Cairo.

Much respect to Linda and her daughter Kelsey as well as her children.

To all the long lost family wherever you are my are frequencies forever lock together and rest in eternal peace to my family & friends I love you dearly.

A loving family is a treasure from your creator If life has blessed you with a close-knit, supportive clan, offer a word of thanks to your Creator because they have given you one of the most precious earthly possessions. ... And it's your responsibility to praise your mother and father for that gift-and to act accordingly.

Being a family means you are a part of something very wonderful. It means you will love and be loved for the rest of your life." "The family is the first essential cell of human society." "Family and friends are hidden treasures, seek them out and enjoy their riches.

Family is important because it provides love, support and a framework of values to each of its members. Family members teach each other, serve one another and share life's joys and sorrows. ... From their first moments of life, children depend on parents and family to protect them and provide for their needs.

Anthropologists generally classify most family organizations as matrifocal (a mother and her children); patrifocal (a father and his children); conjugal (a wife, her husband, and children, also called the nuclear family); avuncular (for example, a grandparent, a brother, his sister and her children), or extended family. In the context of family love, the term refers to bonds characterized by deep affection, respect, loyalty, and healthy attachment. Family relationships are different from other types of bonds. The following characteristics of family love set it apart from other types of love relationships.

An for many people "Family means having someone to love you unconditionally despite you and your shortcomings.

Family is loving and supporting one another even when it's not easy to do so. It's being the best person you could be so that you may inspire your loved ones. Family doesn't see colour, race, creed not culture it sees the heart.

So for every family on the planet, the memories that we make with our family & loved ones is everything." "In a time of test, family is best." "My family is my life, and everything else comes second as far as what's important to me." "Rejoice with your family tell them you love them hug and wish for all your families health to be forever blessed & for those faces to forever smile & be happy in this beautiful world we call life.

At the same time, we humans share biologies, cultures, fashions, art, and media, and so perhaps it is not surprising that we also tend to find beauty in similar things like sunsets, roses and facial symmetrical. ... Beauty can be subjective and yet have a positive value that makes it worth sharing with others. Plus Honesty: being truthful and sincere. Integrity: sticking to your moral and ethical principles and values. Kindness: being considerate and treating others well. Perseverance: persisting in a course of action, belief or purpose. Family values.

Values give families an outlook on life, a way to view the world and their situation as well as an identity. Values can also add to relationships and influence judgments, behaviours, and parenting styles.

Family values serve as the core of what family members do the opinions they have.

Top row, left to right: Rumal Grossman, Aaron Grossman and Natalie Grossman.

Bottom row, left to right: Tyhea Kaur, Jacqueline Grossman

Tyhea on Rumal's shoulders

Aaron and sister
Natalie as kids

Left to right:
Naomi Wilks,
Tyrah Wilks,
Leah Wilkes,
Aaron, Natalie
Grossman

Left to right:
Amara Jones,
Azai Grossman,
Lavae
Grossman,
Tyhea
Kaur, Reign
Grossman

Aaron, Azai
and Lavae

Azai and Lavae

Left to right:
Nana Margaret,
Auntie Annie
and Auntie Lilly,
Dublin, late
60's-early 70's

CHAPTER FOUR

Education. Choices & Decisions.

Plymouth Grove Primary School. Opened in 1906, this imposing red brick school sits on the south side of Plymouth Grove West. This was the first school I attended from the age of three being in nursery with my sister Natalie. This also is the school that my cousins Naomi Leah Tyrah attended before I was even born in the early 1980's so the same pattern of schooling for me and my sister was similar I guess.

I remember being at this school for a few reasons that stand out for me.

One being the assembly they held first thing in the morning like some religious ritual singing lines from old Mc Donald had a farm and blah blah blah black sheep with a bottle of fresh silver cased sealed milk with a straw stuck through the top.

It was here at Plymouth grove where I had found the love for music and the sounds they created one of the first instruments I picked up and played was the flute and

I took a liking to it plus the piano and as infants when the school held little events I got to star in a few musical shows.

My sister is three years older than me so our teachings were different but she assisted me and looked after me not only at playtime on the school grounds but within the school itself.

I got on well at school as far back as I can remember I enjoyed going to school when I was a kid just because there were certain friends that I had a good bond with so as a child it's all about creating and having fun playing games and learning interactive skills off communication understanding how things work whether that's engaging in conversations getting taught what your interests are and what makes your brain tick or just simply from observing the world around you.

I can't remember too much of my days in school as a child especially being the age I was at three/four years old so my mental memory isn't quite strongly connected enough to go back thirty years and tell you in detail specifically.

I can just remember the little bits that stand out for me because my childhood memory's especially at Plymouth Grove school it was good mental exercise and an experience.

Fast forward a year or two when I reached the age of five years old and that's when my decision making started to get a little erratic my attention span was just so limited I fell off playing and liking the musical instruments I once found so attractive in school became a place I deemed as a child's prison.

The reason I say that is because even at an early age I had a problem with authority and not having my way and I thought the only person that has authority over me and should tell me what to do was my beloved mum so because of that ignorance I carried my energy for school became distracted so I went to school thinking that this place is nothing other than a type of big playground complex for me to do what I liked without the repercussions of my mum telling me off or her not seeing what I was doing in school what was only considered as a mischievous adventurous energetic kid with a lot of energy to burn.

At this early stage of my young life, my childhood was nothing other than excitement and being inquisitive.

As I think back and rewind my mind to that era of time from what I told you in my first chapter of (WHAT I REMEMBER) there was no authority from a male figure for a young man to be kept on that path of righteousness therefore my behaviour wasn't tackled properly in the way that it should off been. Don't get me wrong I had aunties and other adults that I was around who would put me in check if I had an attitude or I done something out of character those people were there to correct me but because it was mainly females that I grew up around I did get away with a lot so I guess you can say I took advantage of the fact that I could slip the net and get away with certain things because they had a soft spot for me.

There were only three males that stand out for me at the time that I saw frequently when I was growing up who I consider I was kind of raised by and who I looked up to very much.

Warren who I mentioned in the first chapter who was my auntie Caroline's boyfriend David Todd my auntie Julie's other half and last but not least my mum's boyfriend Trevor Dailey.

I looked up to all three as role models as they all showed me nothing but love and attention but me and Trevor I had a different connection I loved that guy a great deal he didn't just become a good role model in my young life he became my mentor my guardian the one that I felt most comfortable with I had much respect for Trevor "sly" Dailey.

Rest in eternal peace.

I can say that Trevor was the father I never had he taught me a lot even though it went in one ear and out the other because being young I was ignorant and couldn't be told thinking I knew it all so it was hard for me to listen because I did have a little attitude but the words he spoke made sense so I listened to him at times because he did have time for me and he took his time out to give me knowledge which he didn't have to do so I can't appreciate enough for the time I spent with him may the angels protect his soul and forever be at peace.

One thing that I will always remember about Trevor is that he never let us go without him he always had my mum back in many ways he was a real genuine man with a spiritual soul and a good heart.

That's the main reason I felt Trevor was more of a father figure because I was seeing him frequently instead of my biological one which can only be understood from people male/female who has been in that situation and I'm sure plenty of kids around the world have grown up going through similar feelings being in that position. Unfortunately for me Trevor sadly passed away due to a brain haemorrhage that he was suffering from for a long time but it's something I was oblivious to and never knew he was fighting a disease that eventually would cost him his life maybe I was too young to understand what he was going through so I can only imagine how he must off been feeling himself inside at the time but considering he was always happy and smiling you wouldn't think that anything was wrong with him he still had his long Jamaican Rasta locks was in such good shape strong with an athlete's physique.

Trevors death was the pinnacle moment in my young life which had a damaging effect on the way I started to operate life my behaviour started to deteriorate and be a bit more erratic from the smallest minor things like jumping over into peoples gardens getting chased out for pinching footballs or bikes than too eventually throwing little pebble stones at taxi cars a buses cyclists and smashing windows on empty boarded-up homes in the community.

I remember one time at Plymouth Grove primary school the teacher confiscating one of my favourite cartoon character figures called (MODO) from the children's tv series (BIKER MICE FROM MARS) that I snuck into school one morning.

She confiscated (MODO) and told me she's going to hand it to my mum after school I must off be about 6 - 7 years old and I can just remember me being so angry and frustrated that she took it off me and I was so adamant that I was going to retrieve my figure back regardless of anything.

That very same day after school I walked back to the school when it was closed and I knew around five in the evening is roughly when all the teachers' cars had gone and the only concern that I had was getting clocked by the caretaker but he wasn't anywhere to be seen so I pursued with my mission to retrieve (MODO).

My classroom was situated at the rear side of the building the surrounding fence had pointing black spiked arrows sticking up but it was easy for me to climb up and hop over into the school grounds without injuring myself.

The windows they had was like wired glass double glazing stuff didn't shatter like normal glass because the wiring was kind of thick so a house brick or a piece of thick concrete was the only way to penetrate the glass, I hit the window with force 3 - 4 times with this piece of concrete slab hitting and concentrating on the same target to create a bigger hole for me to put my hand through to lift the catch up that was keeping the window secure.

I put my hand through to lift the catch up and as I have done that a piece of the wire within the glass just ripped my right forearm like a piece of paper, the sight of my blood squirting out dramatically like a running tap had me panicking the pain wasn't too bad it just looked very messy and it wasn't nice to look at either.

I ran off from the scene leaving a trail of blood through the car park which didn't stop leaking until I got home, I burst through the door shouting to my mum that I'd just had an accident my mum immediately starts panicking because of the seriousness of the cut wrapped up my arm and rushed me out the door to the nearest A&E.

She rushed me to St Mary's the Royal Infirmary hospital where I was told to give an account on how I got my injury but I just said I'd slipped and fell and landed on a piece of broken glass, they stitched me back together and was given antibiotics to fight off any unwanted infections and to ease the pain and swelling and was sent on my way and made to relax for about a week until the stitches came out it pissed me off because I was out of commission couldn't do the things I'd normally do it was frustrating very much and to add insult to injury I didn't even get (MODO) back.

I never told my mum what happened that day I just remember telling her some bullshit story about how I cut it on a piece of glass that I was playing within an abandoned house similar to what I said to the hospital but little did I know the school had CCTV and saw me throwing this big piece of slab against the window to smash it and could see me entering and then running off a moment's later holding my arm because I've just injured myself trying to break in the school after hours. Because of my age, the police couldn't do anything to prosecute me apart from worn me and issue a caution which is a slap on the wrist and a clip round the ear of my mum but the school on the other hand expelled me for the second or third time my thought process and behaviour was getting worse.

All these complaints that I was receiving from an early age from the school, police, housing associations, even the neighbourhood writing bad reports to the social services and the education department which lead them to build a case on me as well as my mum because they held my mum accountable for my actions and behaviour because of my age.

I can recall them even sending my mum a few letters of acknowledgement about my behaviour a good couple of times explaining how it was effectively affecting my education and learning and she could end up getting prosecuted and taken to court. The process from that point was unknown to me that it wasn't going to be long before those people in authority have some plans for me but it wasn't quite registering in my brain what was inevitably and eventually going to happen.

It was the year off 1992 well 29/12/92 to be exact when Trevor passed I remember it like it was yesterday because it was four days after Christmas and he would normally do his little rounds after he's already been round on Christmas Day.

Christmas is a special day for most especially for kids so it was a bit odd that I never saw him for a few days and because I never saw him until I was told by my mum that Trevor had passed away it was a really big shock to the system for me and a bit too much for my young brain to process & handle at that time because remember I already knew about death due to my auntie Margaret Morgan passing and her funeral was the very first I ever went too so it brought a flood off weird and negative thoughts right back.

From that moment my attitude and my attention span for school took a turn for the worst which then gave the headmaster Mr Congleton no choice but to expel me from Plymouth Grove.

Getting expelled from Plymouth Grove primary school a considerable amount of times at around the age of 5-6 they knew something had to do so they organised another placement for me in Webster primary school.

Before I was transferred and they found me a placement at Webster primary school I had a few months in St. John's primary school while a placement was awaiting me. St John's CofE Primary School is located in Longsight, Manchester and falls under the local authority of Manchester. The school's religious denomination is the Church of England. This mixed-sex primary school has 493 pupils, with a capacity of 472, aged from three up to eleven, and the type of establishment is a voluntary controlled school. The school has 12 teachers with each teacher on average earning the full-time equivalent of £40,650. The most recent Ofsted inspection was on 3rd October 2017 resulting in a satisfactory rating.

I can't tell you anything exciting about being at this school apart from they had bikes and a different set up to Plymouth Grove primary school. It was on the same street which I grew up on between the ages of infant to primary around eight because my mum was moving from house to house for a good few years so it's hard to keep track of where we were exactly at that time but I can say we were in Longsight somewhere.

Webster Primary School is now a three-form entry community school for children aged five to eleven years old and has nursery places for three and four-year-olds. The school is housed in a single-storey building that opened in 1973 and a two-storey building added in 2018 with playgrounds and fields to the side and rear of the school.

People think they've only been open since the seventies. Well, they're right, if they mean the 1870's. Ever heard of Webster Street School? Did you know that they once had a playground...on the roof?!

It was still a concern for the people behind the scenes who made those decisions about my position in schools because of my none compliance whatsoever with the authority of teachers. Due to many complaints by different people within organisations like the local council my mum was constantly receiving letters saying she's liable for prosecution for my behaviour whether that was not going to school or getting picked up by the police for any reason.

I just didn't like getting told what to do and my temper got the better off me when I was approached or stopped from what I liked to do I just didn't like the word (NO).

While the other kids were engaging with the teachers listening and learning I always decided to do the opposite wanting to do my own thing and that's where the difficulties were for the teachers because I was just hard to control they didn't know how to handle me I was deemed as a problem child with learning difficulties and behavioural issues who needed one and one tutoring attendants instead of being in a class with the rest of the kids because they felt that would help me focus more on my education. So then they tried to work with me on my own to help me try to engage more with work but I just didn't like the education I rebelled against the system of education. Plus I also felt the teachers at the time were a bit authoritative harsh and I thought they spoke to me in a way that I didn't like made me feel uncomfortable like I was always picked on couldn't do much to entertain myself unless it was with the teachers felt being watched all the time but now I know it was the monitoring process of my behaviour being challenged.

It wasn't like that for me in my mind back then It was just me thinking I'm being controlled I wasn't hearing anything I was simply not paying attention to anything or anyone maybe you can say I had difficulty controlling my emotions and temper which did lead to my thought process being impaired which would come with negative effects so my behaviour was challenging not only for the teachers but for my mum too she even started seeing a big change in my behaviour.

Moving forward I lasted no longer than six months before I was transferred from Webster primary to Claremont which was a mile down the road in the Manchester Moss Side/Rusholme area.

At that period, I think my mum was in the process of wanting to move from the area we were in nevertheless all the complaints Manchester council was receiving neighbours constantly accusing me saying I'm causing a problem for them and being a nuisance neighbour anything that went wrong in the surrounding community I was to blame the finger would always be pointed at me regardless of me not even playing out police randomly knocking on my mum's door asking questions because somebody's property's been vandalised anything and everything would be an excuse for the police to come knocking on my mum's door. My mum got served an eviction notice by the Manchester council due to my anti-social behaviour and I remember there was one woman that I'll her forget called (LINDA) neighbourhood watcher someone we used to call a curtain twitcher. She had eyes on anything that worked as a community rep for the council so anything that happened whether it was a crime to the joyriders kids hanging on the block smoking weed she would take pictures for evidence & report it to the authorities. I remember the police threatened my mum with prison because the most serious cases of antisocial behaviour that I was involved in was then dealt with by a Criminal behaviour order. Anyone breaching an order will be guilty of a criminal offence. The maximum penalty for this will be five years' imprisonment for adults and up to two years' detention and training for under 18s. But because I was underage it was my mum having to pick up the pieces and deal with the negative effects of my behaviour from the authorities. I started smoking weed because I'd see the older kids out chilling congregating am I was always intrigued by the smell and I knew it wasn't cigarettes because my mum smoked and I could tell the difference between the two.

What was funny about smoking weed is that I was intrigued by the smell all the time because I'd go to my mate's house (BILLY) his dad used to sell it so I was around criminal behaviour and noticed what others were doing so that's when I first started smoking (HASH) (SPUDNICK) it was known but you had to be careful when smoking it because of the hot rocks it would leave of the spliff an if you got it on your clothes it burn little holes through the material and people especially adults would know you'd been smoking.

After realising and understanding Trevor had passed it felt like my life had slowed right down but my aggression within escalated reaching the age of around eight years old.

Due to Trevor passing it hit me like a ton of bricks and in my personal opinion it's not only that he was my mum's boyfriend it's because he was very close to me and to the rest of the family so my emotional state of mind was unbalanced as well being a child it was difficult for me to overcome or even try not to think about the loss of such a respected and very much loved man.

Life didn't get any easier for me because I deemed life not the same without Trevor I couldn't get into any situation without showing some sort of aggression towards humans or smashing something up causing thousands & thousands of pounds worth of damage.

Thinking back I think it was a coping mechanism that I developed which allowed me to get out my anger instead of talking it seemed aggression was the only way for me to express myself and to let others know how I was feeling when I was frustrated.

Though education is to be believed to be the definition of knowledge where you to learn I felt even as a young man they didn't teach you the right stuff about life itself and your roots your history through literacy & numeracy plays a big part in your life. I do believe a proper and good education is very important for all of us. It facilitates quality learning all through life among people of any age group, caste, creed, religion and region. It is the process of achieving knowledge, values, skills, beliefs, and moral habits. But the main purpose of education is to educate individuals within society, to prepare and qualify them for work in the economy as well as to integrate people into society and teach them the values and morals of society. The role of education is means of socializing individuals and keeping society smoothing and remain stable. Though it was suggested.

Those who get an education have higher incomes, have more opportunities in their lives, and tend to be healthier. Societies benefit as well. Societies with high rates of education completion have lower crime, better overall health, and civic involvement.

Lack of access to education is considered the root of poverty.

Whereas I have seen a child gets the education from his experiences outside the school as well as from those within based on these factors. There are three main types of education, namely, Formal, Informal and Non-formal. Each of these types is discussed below.

Meaning & Types of Education:

Education is a gradual process that brings positive changes in human life and behaviour. We can also (DEFINE EDUCATION) as "a process of acquiring knowledge through study or imparting the knowledge by way of instructions or some other practical procedure".

What is education?

My thoughts on Educational programming; I believe education brings a natural and lasting change in an individual's reasoning and ability to achieve the targeted goal.

It facilitates us to investigate our considerations and thoughts and makes it ready to express them in various shapes.

Education is the main thing that encourages us to distinguish between right and wrong because in the absence of education, we can't do what we need or we can't achieve our goal.

Straightforwardly, we can say, "education is the passage to progress". It is additionally the way to our fate as achievements can only be accomplished when individuals have information, aptitudes, and frame of mind.

In this way, education resembles a medium through which we can associate with various individuals and offer our thoughts.

To tackle issues and do inventiveness we first need to gain proficiency with some essential abilities. We require learning and abilities to wind up increasingly imaginative. So education is fundamentally learning of abilities and ideas that can make us increasingly innovative and issue solvers. Education is to pick up the capacity to develop and take care of issues to achieve their lawful motives.

Education also means helping people to learn how to do things and encouraging them to think about what they learn.

It is also important for educators to teach ways to find and use information. Through education, the knowledge of society, country, and of the world is passed on from generation to generation.

In democracies, through education, children and adults are supposed to learn how to be active and effective citizens.

More specific, education helps and guide individuals to transform from one class to another. Empowered individuals, societies, countries by education are taking an edge over individuals who stand on the bottom pyramid of growth.

TYPES OF EDUCATION.

Education goes beyond what takes place within the four walls of the classroom.

A child gets the education from his experiences outside the school as well as from those within based on these factors. There are three main types of education, namely, Formal, Informal and Non-formal. Each of these types is discussed below.

Formal Education.

Formal education or formal learning usually takes place in the premises of the school, where a person may learn basic, academic, or trade skills. Small children often attend a nursery or kindergarten but often formal education begins in elementary school and continues with secondary school.

Post-secondary education (or higher education) is usually at a college or university which may grant an academic degree. It is associated with a specific or stage and is provided under a certain set of rules and regulations.

Formal education is given by specially qualified teachers they are supposed to be efficient in the art of instruction. It also observes strict discipline. The student and the teacher both are aware of the facts and engage themselves in the process of education.

Examples of Formal Education.

- Learning in a classroom
- School grading/certification, college, and university degrees
- Planned education of different subjects having a proper syllabus acquired by attending the institution.

Characteristics of formal education.

- Formal education is structured hierarchically.
- It is planned and deliberate.
- Scheduled fees are paid regularly.
- It has a chronological grading system.

- It has a syllabus and is subject-oriented. The syllabus has to be covered within a specific period.
- The child is taught by the teachers

Advantages of Formal education:

- An organized educational model and up to date course contents.
- Students acquire knowledge from trained and professional teachers.
- Structured and systematic learning process.
- Intermediate and final assessments are ensured to advance students to the next learning phase.
- Institutions are managerially and physically organized.
- Leads to a formally recognized certificate.
- Easy access to jobs.

Disadvantages of Formal education:

- Sometimes, brilliant students are bored due to the long wait for the expiry of the academic session to promote to the next stage
- The chance of bad habits' adoption may be alarming due to the presence of both good and bad students in the classroom

- Wastage of time as some lazy students may fail to learn properly despite motivation by the professional trainers.
- Some unprofessional and non-standard education systems may cause the wastage of time and money of the students which leads to disappointment from formal education and argue them to go for non-formal education.
- Costly and rigid education as compare to other forms of learning

Informal Education.

Informal education may be a parent teaching a child how to prepare a meal or ride a bicycle.

People can also get an informal education by reading many books from a library or educational websites.

Informal education is when you are not studying in a school and do not use any particular learning method. In this type of education, conscious efforts are not involved. It is neither pre-planned nor deliberate. It may be learned at some marketplace, hotel or home.

Unlike formal education, informal education is not imparted by an institution such as a school or college. Informal education is not given according to any fixed timetable. There is no set curriculum required. Informal education consists of experiences and living in the family or community.

Examples of Informal Education.

- Teaching the child some basics such as numeric characters.
- Someone learning his/her mother tongue
- A spontaneous type of learning, "if a person standing in a bank learns about opening and maintaining the account at the bank from someone."

Characteristics of Informal Education.

- It is independent of boundary walls.
- It has no definite syllabus.
- It is not pre-planned and has no timetable.
- No fees are required as we get informal education through daily experience and by learning new things.
- It is a lifelong process in a natural way.
- The certificates/degrees are not involved and one has no stress for learning the new things.
- You can get from any source such as media, life experiences, friends, family etc.

Advantages of Informal Education.

- More naturally learning process as you can learn anywhere and at any time from your daily experience.

- It involves activities like individual and personal research on a topic of interest for themselves by utilizing books, libraries, social media, the internet or getting assistance from informal trainers.
- Utilizes a variety of techniques.
- No specific period.
- Less costly and time-efficient learning process.
- No need to hire experts as most of the professionals may be willing to share their precious knowledge with students/the public through social media and the internet.
- Learners can be picked up the requisite information from books, TV, radio or conversations with their friends/family members.

Disadvantages of Informal Education.

- Information acquired from the internet, social media, TV, radio or conversations with friends/family members may lead to disinformation.
- Utilized techniques may not be appropriate.
- No proper schedule/period.
- Unpredictable results are simply the wastage of time.
- Lack of confidence in the learner.
- Absence of discipline, attitude and good habits.

Non-formal Education.

Non-formal education includes adult basic education, adult literacy education or school equivalency preparation.

In nonformal education, someone (who is not in school) can learn literacy, other basic skills or job skills.

Home education, individualized instruction (such as programmed learning), distance learning and computer-assisted instruction are other possibilities.

Non-formal education is imparted consciously and deliberately and systematically implemented. It should be organized for a homogeneous group. Non-formal, education should be programmed to serve the needs of the identified group. This will necessitate flexibility in the design of the curriculum and the scheme of evaluation.

Examples of Non-formal Education.

- Boy Scouts and Girls Guides develop some sports programs such as swimming comes under nonformal education.
- Fitness programs.
- Community-based adult education courses.
- Free courses for adult education developed by some organizations.

Characteristics of Non-formal Education.

- Nonformal education is planned and takes place apart from the school system.
- The timetable and syllabus can be adjustable.
- Unlike theoretical formal education, it is practical and vocational education.
- Nonformal education has no age limit.
- Fees or certificates may or may not be necessary.
- It may be full time or part-time learning and one can earn and learn together.
- It involves learning professional skills.

Advantages of Non-formal Education.

- Practised and vocational training.
- Naturally growing minds that do not wait for the system to amend.
- Literacy with skillfulness growth in which self-learning is appreciated.
- Flexibility in age, curriculum and time.
- The open-ended educational system in which both the public and private sectors are involved in the process.
- No need to conduct regular exams.
- Diplomas, certificates, and awards are not essential to be awarded.

Disadvantages of Non-formal Education.

- The attendance of participants is unsteady.
- Sometimes, it's just a wastage of time as there is no need to conduct the exam on regular basis and no degree/diploma is awarded at the end of the training session.
- Basic reading and writing skills are crucial to learning.
- No professional and trained teachers.
- Students may not enjoy full confidence as the regular students enjoy.
- Some institutes provide fake certification through online courses just for the sake of earning.

Educational disadvantage is demonstrated in many ways, most often in poor levels of participation and achievement in the formal education system. There are other ways in which children may be disadvantaged, for example as a result of a disability, literacy difficulties, ill health, poverty etc.

Due to all the difficulties within my educational progress from primary schools I reached the age of eight and the last mainstream school that would give me a chance was Old Trafford primary school on Stretford Road Manchester.

This is before all the stuff I'd done a few years before like the weed-smoking my attitude being a nuisance and the aggression towards the teachers and other people plus all the police reports and criminal damage in the community the evictions and the court fines (EVERYTHING).

Many factors can contribute to a child feeling angry or expressing anger in challenging ways. Unresolved feelings, such as grief related to a divorce or the loss of a loved one, can be the root of the problem. A history of trauma or experiencing bullying may lead to anger, too.

I can't remember the time gap between moving from Longsight to Rusholme but I know I was 7-8 years old.

Maybe 6-12 months had passed and we moved from Rusholme Great Western ST Manchester that's after getting my mum evicted from Longsight.

We moved to beever street Old Trafford and they put me in Old Trafford junior school where they had a court order in place that stated that Old Trafford junior school was the last stop after all the schools in the Greater Manchester area wouldn't accept me because of my behaviour because when they read my file they saw I needed more attention than the average kids in their school and that is something the school couldn't provide so my mum kept telling me that the government are gonna take me away and there's nothing that she can do.

I continued the bad behaviour disregarding & ignoring the words that my mum was speaking still doing the same shit I was doing a few years prior but my crime got a lot more brazen & reckless.

It was the same pattern walking through the front doors of the school then running out the back It lasted no longer than a few months and the dreaded red pen was out again getting bad reports from school was all the social services needed plus all the police reports from running away from home getting picked up at the age of 9 years old in Manchester's red light District. The chapter (THE STREETZ) (criminals & influences) explains the lead up to why I ended up in care living with strangers.

The 1996 Manchester bombing was an attack carried out by the Provisional Irish Republican Army (IRA) on Saturday 15 June 1996. ... The IRA had sent telephoned warnings about 90 minutes before the bomb detonated.

At least 75,000 people were evacuated from the area, but the bomb squad were unable to defuse the bomb in time.

Summertime mid-afternoon Saturday 15th June 1996 the ground shakes that I'm standing on playing kick-ball against the wall outside my house Deanwell Close Longsight nine days before I just turned aged nine in June 1996.

15/06/1996 the day I will never forget because the sound is still a ringing distant memory and I can still hear the echoes and powerful intensity of the explosion in the back of my head sounding like world war 3 was about to happen 5 miles away from where we lived.

That tragedy on the 15th June 1996 cost the English economy millions plus so many people nearly lost their lives also many shops and independent businesses were destroyed millions off taxpayers money paying for the catastrophic devastating damage left in the aftermath of the bombing which then saw the good and new developments being built in Manchester.

That devastating attack from the I.R.A sticks in my mind like a permanently stained window for many reasons and it's something that I will never forget and I'm sure it's something the Mancunian people won't be in a hurry to forget what happened either on that beautiful summers day what could have turned out a lot worse than it did on June 15 1996.

Not only because it was in my home town of Manchester it mainly because at that time me myself and I was going through a bad stage of behaving as I've explained in this chapter of (EDUCATION) (CHOICES & DECISIONS) from the period of age 5-9 the bad things started manifesting and my young life was spiralling out of control and most certainly changing dramatically which than lead to (CARE) an living with strangers.

My book is intended to give my experiences of how I see things through the my eyes of mine and why I believe we don't always have to play it by the book.

I'm sure many people across the world have or still today see education as part of life and it's something we need not only for the future but it's there as a tool to gain knowledge from especially learning about the things you have no idea about that's why it's good to be taught but on the flip side there is not a problem with anyone or anybody wanting to study for themselves and gain the knowledge in their way whether you read books have conversations with peers watching programs your life is yours your brain is yours and I believe everybody has the right to have a different way of seeing things in life but unfortunately they are laws set in place an were talking about (SCHOOL) which was set through religious organisations dating back in time.

The history of education in England is documented from the Saxon settlement of England, and the setting up of the first cathedral schools in 597 & 604.

EDUCATION IN ENGLAND - remained closely linked to religious institutions until the nineteenth century, although charity schools and "free grammar schools", which were open to children of any religious beliefs, became more common in the early modern period. Nineteenth-century reforms expanded education provision and introduced widespread state-funded schools. By the 1880s education was compulsory for children aged 5 to 10, with the school leaving age progressively raised since then, most recently to 18 in 2015.

The education system was expanded and reorganised multiple times throughout the 20th century, with a Tripartite system introduced in the 1940s, splitting secondary education into grammar schools secondary technical schools and secondary modern schools in the 1960s began to be phased out in favour of comprehensive schools further reforms in the 1980s introduced the National curriculum and allowed parents to choose which school their children went to. Academies were introduced in the 2000s and became the main type of secondary school in the 2010s. I hope many people reading my book gain the knowledge for them to pass on and most importantly gain an understanding of my world and my thoughts and feelings whether that's about educational beliefs, spiritual beliefs or even maybe my religious beliefs it's my opinion, my life and it's a great honour to share it with the world.

CHAPTER FIVE

Trapped In Care.
In The Hands of Strangers.

Along with Ramshaw Rocks and Hen Cloud, they form a gritstone escarpment which is popular with hikers and rock climbers plus free runners It is often very busy especially at weekends.

The Roaches Estate which includes Hen Cloud was purchased by the Peak District National Park Authority in the 1980s to safeguard the area from adverse development. From May 2013 Staffordshire wildlife trust took on the management of the Roaches Estate.

In clear conditions, it is possible to see much of Cheshire and views stretching as far as Snowdon in Wales and Winter Hill in Lancashire.

The Roaches are the most prominent part of a curving ridge that extends for several miles from Hen Cloud in the south to Back Forest and Hangingstone in the north-west. At the top, there is a small pool called Doxey Pool that is, according to legend, inhabited by a water spirit. Nearby are the broad hills of Gun and Morgridge.

The Roaches, as we now know them, from the French for rocks "Roches", was referred to using the Gallic term up until as recently as 100 years ago.

The Schools

Younger pupils (7-12) are educated at a site in the spectacular Peak District National Park between Leek in Staffordshire and Buxton in Derbyshire. The location of the school is delightful. It is located amongst heather-clad moorland and high rocky outcrops. The boarding accommodation for up to 8 pupils is housed in a specially adapted farmhouse in its grounds with tastefully decorated individual study bedrooms and well-equipped facilities for recreation.

The separate classrooms are well furnished and resourced with up to date books and equipment geared to educating the future adult of the 21st Century.

The therapeutic community is comprised of five schools and is peer-assessed through the community of communities network. The three small farm school sites, Old Sams Farm School, Bradshaw School and Evergreen School are designed to help stabilise children in a remote setting to prepare them for a transition to a larger-scale setting.

The roaches (lower end school) opened in 1995 and is part of Care Today, which was founded by Dr Sean Fitzpatrick and Ellen Fitzpatrick. The Roaches School believes in inequality of opportunity for every child. and encourages children to flourish in their ideals and ambitions, offering an environment that promotes freedom of expression.

The Roaches Therapeutic Community has evolved from an ambition to ensure that young people from all sectors of education are offered the best possible chance to engage fully with schooling.

A model for the best ambitions of education, care and therapy has developed into the national philosophy of The Roaches Therapeutic Network.

The Network prides itself on offering high-quality teachers, therapists and residential care professionals to address the needs of complex children in a family-oriented environment.

Care proceedings.

The council can start 'care proceedings' if they're very worried about a child.

They can apply for a 'care order' which means the council will have parental responsibility for your child and can determine where your child can live.

They can apply for a 'placement order' as well if they believe that the child should be adopted. This allows the council to place the child with suitable adopters.

Interim care orders

At the start of care proceedings, the council asks the family court to make a temporary court order, called an 'interim care order'.

If the court agrees, the council can take the child into care temporarily. This can be for up to 8 weeks at first.

Looking at the case

It can take up to 26 weeks for a court to decide what should happen to the child. Some complex cases can take longer.

During this time a social worker, an officer from the Children and Family Court Advisory and Support Service and other people will be trying to understand the reasons why the child may be at risk. They will also look at what can be done to keep them safe.

They will talk to the parents and the child. They may talk to other family members or friends about looking after the child if they cannot safely live at home. The parents might also get support.

Reports

The social worker and other authorities will each write a report for the court. These will outline what they think should happen to the child.

They will include whether they think the child should be taken into the care of or stay with the family.

Once all the information has been gathered, there will be a court hearing.

Section 31 of the Children Act 1989 – Care Order the court can create a care order under Section 31 of the Children Act, placing a child in the care of a designated local authority, with parental responsibility being shared between the parents and the local authority.

This is what was placed on me where my mum still had parental consent and still had a say on what she thought would off been best for me so it wasn't an order where I would off been in the hands of strangers until I was eighteen.

They focused more on The 5 P's of child protection and Prevention, Paramountcy, Partnership, Protection and Parental Responsibility. If it's means anything for your parents out there making your child aware of the 5 Ps for an awkward situation they come across or a situation they may not understand in their life, will be a very good idea it's just for educational purposes.

That's resorting back to many situations I was in when I didn't understand what was being said or what was going on until they came with the authorities and took me away from my family home, I began to start showing symptoms typically beginning in my childhood; the average age of onset is 7 years old.

Obsessive-compulsive disorder (OCD) and posttraumatic stress disorder (PTSD) are closely related to anxiety disorders, which some may experience at the same time, along with depression.

This explains why around the age of seven after I already lost Trevor the thought of me having (PTSD) at that early age wasn't thought of and taken into consideration because naturally childhood trauma of any kind usually results in anxiety disorders and even depression.

I didn't understand what depression was until I found myself at the age of nine years old being taken away from my family and the life that I only knew was suddenly ripped away from me. It was difficult adapting to the new way of life being in the care I couldn't handle the fact that it had happened to me I had been taken away from everything I've ever known.

I can remember the day they came for me police liaison officers and uniformed police officers & the social services with the care staff which was accompanying me back to the establishment they had arranged which was the Roaches farm lower school for children with similar issues & problems like myself.

It wasn't that easy for the authorities to escort me to where I was being sent, I was kicking punching and screaming crying telling my mum I didn't want to go police grabbing me as I'm trying to make off down the street my sister with tears in her eyes it wasn't a good day my little brother was around 2 years old so he didn't know what was happening.

I was holding on to anything I could latch onto but then they'd pull my fingers so I'd loosen my grip and I can honestly say at that moment it felt like I was being taken away forever never to return to my family like I was getting abducted the feeling was unbearable I wouldn't wish that on my worst enemy especially a child.

They tried to make my journey a better one by having my mum in tow travel with us so I didn't feel alone and lost with strangers but still in the car I was not having it I was trying to lift the handbrake slapping the staff threatening to spit in their faces my emotions was all fucked up I actually couldn't believe what was happening to me it was hard for me to comprehend but you can only imagine at the age of nine years old being taken away from your family home to be placed in an establishment with other kids that you don't even know plus you know the atmosphere and the world is different to what you understand and know best I didn't know what to expect getting lead into an unknown world.

We drove for which felt like hours at the time and I could just feel this not unpleasant feeling running through my body something I've never felt before it was a weird moment my eyes constantly observing the road signs trying to figure out where they were taking me.

All I remember is after leaving the main roads and trying to read the signs I blinked and we were in no man's land all I could see was scenes of greenery big hills for miles 100 foot trees and stoned Roman fencing around the perimeters of the landscape I have to say it was a beautiful scene but it wasn't a holiday trip this was real and it was the first time my eyes have ever seen live animals like cows, sheep's, horses, lambs, goats, lama's, chickens and this is all on the mainland as were driving up some long path designed only to get to your destination of the care home other than that it's all private land with some footpaths open to the public.

We drove down this narrow road full of gravel and in the distance I could see this little house situated on its own with the smoke coming out the chimney big as we drove in closer to the house we were stopped by one big metal farm gate where one member of staff had to jump out and undo the lock to let our drive-in.

My emotions were still all over the place heart beating fast but controlled maybe because my mum was there with me plus my sister I felt a little bit at ease but the time went on I was a bit more relaxed by the time we pulled up to our destination anyway. I was greeted and welcomed by other staff members and other kids as I stepped out of the car and walked through these wooden doors into this farmhouse I was still unsure and feeling a bit out of place and my mum only stayed for like an hour while they tried to settle me in but I didn't want my mum to go and I wanted to go back with her and my sister but I was there feeling trapped and I knew it wasn't going to happen and that was the start of my journey through the care system. I was demoralised and I think it was down to the seriousness of my situation the symptoms for demoralization include the severity of illness, diminished functional ability, past depression, trait anxiety, younger age, poor family cohesion and quality of relationships, avoidant or confrontational coping style, weak environmental mastery, ... most of these things contributed for the way I was feeling especially having past depression & anxiety of losing Trevor at a very young age. It was a very big change In my young life back in 1996 I was dealing with a lot of stressful and difficult situations especially being a child I was suffering from the main 7 causes of stress?

- I found myself under lots of pressure.
- I was facing big changes.

- worrying about my family and myself and what's going to happen to me.
- not having much or any control over the outcome of the situation I was in.
- having responsibilities that I was finding overwhelming.
- At first, I wasn't having enough work, activities and it wasn't easy adapting to the change in my life.
- times was off uncertainty.

The day my mum left me at the roaches farm, till this day I can still picture the cloud of dust from the gravel as she left for the journey back home to Manchester. I was in a depressed state of mind my mindset was fucked up I was trying my best to soak up the weird atmosphere around me but I was struggling and I found it weird that the other kids my age were running around like they were happy and like they had no care or worries in the world it was a crazy feeling.

The peak age for my anxiety kicked in between the ages of 5-7 years old but in some cases, it may start at adolescence. However, everyone is different, and your anxiety can peak at various times, depending on what triggers it initially. Merely feeling anxious is the body's response to danger as the fight-or-flight hormone kicks in. Anxiety may present as fear or worry, but it can also make children irritable and angry.

Anxiety symptoms can also include trouble sleeping, as well as physical symptoms like fatigue, headaches, or stomachaches. Some anxious children keep their worries to themselves and, thus, the symptoms can be missed. I found it hard to settle for a long time and I never slept well for months literally around 6 months I had trouble relaxing in that environment and the most fucked up part was the fact that if I did go to sleep I would have dreams about being at home and wake up knowing I'm far away from being where I was supposed to be it wasn't a nice feeling. The care home had rules and regulations that you had to follow like times for lights out/bedtime & eat food times when you'd have to get up and get ready for your breakfast in the morning before starting education or any other activities.

It was hard adjusting to the routine coming from what my life was like I found it hard to obey the rules and regulations I couldn't adjust to that way of life especially having a problem with getting told what to do by people I didn't know I couldn't cope with it. I didn't listen to anyone I still had a major problem with my mum signing her signature on the dotted line and agreeing to put me in care not realising at that time it was down to my behaviour but I was angry, frustrated, irate, annoyed, cross, vexed, irritated, aggrieved, resentful, infuriated, in a temper, incensed, raging, incandescent, wrathful, fuming, ranting, raving, seething, all their emotions were running deep within.

Anger is an emotion characterized by antagonism toward someone or something you feel has deliberately done you wrong. Anger can be a good thing. It can give you a way to express negative feelings, for example, or motivate you to find solutions to problems.

I didn't want to find any solutions to fix my position I was angry and very upset about being where I was I couldn't cope with being looked after by strangers I felt my mum had done me wrong I felt she didn't love me I was an emotional wreck at nine years old depressed & stressed thinking all kinds of crazy shit thinking suicidal thoughts my young brain was in a very dark zone.

Plus at the same time it didn't help seeing crazy shit from the other kids that had more mental health issues than I did some kids had serious issues kids from all walks of life and what makes it scary was that even though we were only children most of us there was education enough to understand and streetwise enough because of the life we already had before ending up in care. Mental disorders among children are described as serious changes in the way children typically learn, behave, or handle their emotions, which cause distress and problems getting through the day. My days consisted of running away all the time the local authorities looking for me in the woods and highlands I didn't know where I'd be going but all that's in my mind is trying to find the Buxton train station because over time I discovered and learned the geography of my surroundings. I'd get caught a few times because I'd get lost and end up in somebody's farming land and a little mixed-race boy wandering the wilderness of the Peak District was a bit of sight to see for most people but the people that lived within the landscape of the Peak District knew of the care home an already knew that I'd be from there the police would be called and I'd always get brought back to the home but not without kicking and punching and trying to fight police and staff I was hard to handle they found it hard to control and restrain me I was a handful. Because of my temper and my explosive aggression in the end they set up a soft room called the (THE PADDED BOX) so when I'd be brought back from running away or getting ready to start smashing things up they'll restrain me and put me in there with padded shapes for me to throw kick/punch and take my anger out on.

They'd leave me in there until they felt it's safe for me to come out again and they were happy I've calmed down because they said I was a threat to the other kid's and they needed to protect their safety plus the members of staff after a few incidents of my outburst requested for a medical treatment assessment to be done and the assessment they did displayed signs of (A.D.H.D) another behavioural problem.

There was a couple of times that I did make it back to Manchester, made it back to Old Trafford a good few times by sneaking on the train and hiding in between the two carriage chairs so when the ticket man came he couldn't see me. The hard part about that was when we'd stop at Manchester Piccadilly station you have to show your ticket to the guard at the exit for him to let you through so what I used to do is walk next to a lady or man like I'm with them and they wouldn't blink an eye and that's the only way I could have got through otherwise I was fucked. Soon as I'd land in Manchester I'd go straight to Rusholme to check my closest homeboy (Zico "C-Loc" Reid) he'd be happy to see me because it would off been months since we saw each other and it wouldn't take long before we were hanging out of somebody's taxi robbing their stuff pouches of money in change and banknotes, mobile phones, car stereos, anything we could turn into cash we'd have to take it was called a (SMASH & GRAB).

We'd buy weed & munchies and just sit at his grandma's house (Aunt Kate) listening to music and smoking till we passed out, I'd be wanted by the police for absconding from the care home and I'd avoid capture for about 2-3 days then get caught then get brought back to the roaches farm.

I was diagnosed with (conduct disorder).

Conduct Disorder (CD) is diagnosed when children show an ongoing pattern of aggression toward others, and serious violations of rules and social norms at home, in school, and with peers. These rule violations may involve breaking the law and result in arrest. Children with CD are more likely to get injured and may have difficulties getting along with peers.

Examples of CD behaviours include

- Breaking serious rules, such as running away, staying out at night when told not to, or skipping school
- Being aggressive in a way that causes harm, such as bullying, fighting, or being cruel to animals
- Lying, stealing, or damaging other people's property on purpose.

I was one of those kids that sometimes was happy but had mixed emotions and at times wanted to argue when I didn't get my way, I was aggressive, or I acted in anger & defiant around adults.

A behaviour disorder may be diagnosed when these disruptive behaviours are uncommon for the child's age at the time, persist over time, or are severe. Because disruptive behaviour disorders involve acting out and showing unwanted behaviour towards others they are often called externalizing disorders.

Mental health and substance misuse can cause disorders and affect people from all walks of life and all age groups. These illnesses are common, recurrent, and often serious, but they are treatable and many people do recover. Mental disorders involve changes in thinking, mood, and/or behaviour. These disorders can affect how we relate to others and make choices. Reaching a level that can be formally diagnosed often depends on a reduction in a person's ability to function as a result of the disorder. For example:

- For people under the age of 18, the term "Serious Emotional Disturbance" refers to a diagnosable mental, behavioural, or emotional disorder which results in functional impairment that substantially interferes with or limits the child's role or functioning in the family, school, or community activities.
- Substance use disorders occur when the recurrent use of alcohol and/or drugs causes clinically significant impairment, including health problems, disability, and failure to meet major responsibilities at work, school, or home.

All that smoking weed plus the dysfunctional negativity from what I was seeing also doing don't forget I wasn't enticed by anyone or being pressured by older peers it was just me simply being adventurous wanting to discover and see the world for myself.

Being in that (PADDED BOX) affected me it did the best way to describe it is probably a feeling what a prisoner feels like being locked in a box for a considerable amount of time there's nothing more damaging for a child to go through. Despite my anger being out of control, it was their way of feeling like they had control over me because restraining me only resulted in them getting kicked & punched or maybe even an object being thrown. They created & designed that (PADDED BOX) especially for me because they weren't many kids that had that same problem they were quieter and reserved there were a few accusations where the staff had to use the box for other kids but it was considered a last resort type punishment. Because of my behaviour and the way I was acting from the day my mum left I never saw her again for a straight six months and that had a major effect on the way my thought process was and because of the time scale that I was separated from my family I started to be more rebellious against the system and that period is when I started having mix feelings about my mums love for me and why she felt the need to place me in care it took a while for me to understand her position as a mother because it must off been very hard for any mother having to sign their child over to any authority.

There was a little red phone that I used to use to phone my mum on and I remember it had been a good few months since I'd been at the farmhouse I hadn't seen or spoken to her properly which felt like an eternity. I would use that phone constantly every day repeatedly saying to mum I want to come back home and I'll be good I'll behave myself and go to school the words of response from my mum finally hit home when she replied "there's nothing I can son it's out of my hands" I didn't realise at that point it was going to be a painful process that I had to go through to get back home which was to start showing the social services and any other type of authorities that I can behave an go to school like a normal child she explained my situation to me where I understood but couldn't quite understand why she couldn't have just come to pick me up so it played on my mind for a long time a very long time.

Few months had passed when I started relaxing a bit more adapting to the new way of life chosen for me which was out of my control I was more streetwise enough to understand that I had to adapt and start working towards getting back home where I belong.

Tina Taylor a member of staff who worked with me took a liking to me and kind of mothered me she saw something different in me regardless of my behaviour she knew with a bit off T.L.C she could get through to me and get my attention in certain ways and because she treated me differently to any other members in authority that I'd ever come across I trusted her I liked her we got on well I had my moments of frustration plus my bad days but I was more reserved when Tina was on duty probably because I had a lot of respect for her she reinstalled some love back into my heart and my troubled world.

She was a good woman always good to be around she had very strong characteristics and had a positive energy about her I'm not sure if she was married at the time but I know she cared a great deal for me I'll never forget her and the way she was with me it was good to know that people I didn't know actually cared it was heartwarming she even took me on my first holiday to Malaga, Spain when I was nine years old with her family it was a good experience.

The largest city on the Costa del Sol, Malaga has a typical Mediterranean climate and is also known as the birthplace of the famous Spanish artist Pablo Picasso. The city offers beaches, hiking, architectural sites, art museums, excellent shopping and cuisine. I remember the hotel we were staying at I wandered off in the building and came across those vending machines that hold drinks crisps and all that sorts of stuff I remember it being open for some reason and I started helping myself to the contents of all these Spanish drinks and crisps plus they sold cigarettes and I was just grabbing all sorts and stuffing them down my pants.

I made off not only to get caught by Tina with all the stuff in my bag it wasn't a good look for me after she organised to take me away with the family plus CCTV caught me and I had to return all the things it was funny for me at the time but not so funny for Tina because

I think she was made to pay for the stuff I took otherwise our stay at the hotel resort would be terminated.

She didn't find the cigarettes as I had them in my pocket and only took two boxes of embassy number 1 plus I used to smoke them on the hotel resorts grounds because where we stayed was gated off and separate from the normal public.

I used to sneak the beer from the fridge (San Miguel) of Tina's other half and drink that on the balcony watching over the beautiful scenery of Malaga with a cigarette like I was 29 years old it was amazing "I felt like I was a grown-ass man" taking liberties I was when you think back poor old Tina and her family putting up with my bullshit on a family holiday could only be me so my apologies Tina and thank you so much for your time and patience with me your a good soul I'll never forget what you have done for me from the heart. Many other members of staff gave me their time and tried their best to make me see things differently and what they would say is don't think my mum doesn't love me anymore because I'm here because she does it's just a difficult situation but in time you'll understand. Those words from Tina and many others that knew my situation stuck with me and I started to engage more with education and wasn't running away as much as I did when I first got there after say the 6 months trial process I could get to go home to see my family every week for a few hours than I'd have to return to the home the same day. It was nice to start getting to see my world again like friends and family every week but another thing that was damaging for me at that time was the more I got to go home the more I got used to it and before I knew it I was running off from members of staff that would be taking me back to the home because I just couldn't take being there anymore especially only having two-hour visits. I refused to go back to the home a good few times because I hated leaving my family home then having to go back to the farmhouse it was messing with my head and make my situation worse sometimes if my behaviour would be bad during the week coming up to going home they'd say I'm not allowed to go this week because they feel I'm not in the right frame-off mind and it would only affect my emotions. This was a very big flip side to that decision they would make on my behalf because that didn't go down well with me whatsoever the dreaded (PADDED BOX) was awaiting me because I'd start smashing the place up uncontrollably fly off into an angry rage.

I'd have to go through this procedure a dozen times a week maybe even 4/5 times a month my behaviour didn't get any better but the only good thing was my mum still had a say in what happened to me and she didn't like the idea of the (PADDED BOX) but they explained that it was for my best interest because my temper gets out off control and it's their way of preventing me assaulting staff hurting myself or worse the other kids.

Education played a big part in what I had to do to achieve going home every week I had to earn so many points to be granted permission to go home so because in time I discovered that's what position they had me in I started trying to monopolise certain things but it was hard going against the system I'd always come unstuck.

It took me a while to realise that the more I fought against the system was the more time I spent away from my natural world because I believed I didn't belong in care living with strangers, I started to do more educational stuff and it was weird because where we have done our education in a small cabin type shack with a generator on the farm grounds powering the computers other electrical equipment. I'm not too sure but don't quote me on this as it was 25 - 26 years ago but I think the actual home itself ran off the generator everything relied on that big generator I can recall a few times the generator would stop working and we would have to use candles and wait for the next morning for the engineers to come out and fix it especially in the wintertime the weather was craziest up in the high mountain hills.

My stay at the lower school wasn't that much of a heartbreaking time for me when I think back but it was a very difficult time especially as a child being in that position because it was for all the wrong reasons plus it didn't help to see what I've seen due to the mental health that others had to deal with and as a child, you shouldn't have to witness and be in those traumatic situations because they stick with you forever.

There were kids there that did need therapy kids that came from broken homes where they've been traumatised through child neglect sexual abused children that were all messed up in the head orphans that had no parents it was like a children's asylum it was crazy.

After say 12 to 18 months my time was due to end because I was coming up to secondary school and once you reach the age of eleven you move on to the higher school in Biddulph Stoke on Trent.

Fairhaven.

I was transferred to Fairhaven the older school where pupils (11-16) are educated at the Upper School site near Biddulph in Staffordshire, with on-site residence for up to 10 pupils. The school is located in a large Grade 2 listed building with extensive grounds. Again, the standards of accommodation and education facilities are high and the unit for the older pupils is geared to preparing the young people for independent living and nationally recognised qualifications when they leave the school. The emphasis throughout is the provision of quality care and education.

Now, this is where my life started to take a different turn because Fairhaven housed older kids from different walks of life and kids there had more of a troubled past and were more difficult to control to me it felt like a breeding ground for upcoming criminals.

Kids coming from or on their way to secure units ended up there even kids with mental health issues there was a mixed variety of people different set up from being at the lower school the atmosphere was more intense.

There were alcoholics at 15-16 but as they say, children and young people are advised not to drink alcohol before the age of 18. Alcohol use during the teenage years is related to a wide range of health and social problems. However, if children do drink alcohol underage, it shouldn't be until they are at least 15. Plus there were drug-taking people from outside the home who would know people in the home and visit them to smoke weed and drink alcoholic drinks outside the grounds you could smell the aroma from cannabis lingering.

They say that the teenage brains are still developing, and alcohol can cause permanent damage to areas that control judgment, impulse control, and memory. Teens are more likely to binge drink (four to five or more drinks at a time) when they consume alcohol. This can lead to unplanned sexual activity, violence, and alcohol poisoning. This explains my theory of impaired ability to make decisions when of the influence of drugs and drink your not capable of acting in the right way violence breaks out because I've seen a few fights from the 15-16-year-olds that was under the influence and it didn't go down well, it's not a good sight for a young man to see. They say Youth violence increases the risk for behavioural and mental health difficulties, including future violence perpetration and victimization, smoking, substance use, obesity, high-risk sexual behaviour, depression, academic difficulties, school dropout, and suicide. Youth violence affects entire communities. Plus there are many consequences that will include increased incidences of depression, anxiety, posttraumatic stress disorder, and suicide; increased risk of cardiovascular disease; and premature mortality.

The health consequences of violence vary with the age and sex of the victim as well as the form of violence. At the age of eleven, the things I saw behind the closed doors of Fairhaven was very depressing and stressful and just being around that sort of atmosphere wasn't good for a child to be around it was very different from being at the lower school the roaches was more secure and controlled Fairhaven you was free to roam so took advantage of the freedom I was given especially after being stuck on that farmhouse for a few years it was refreshing. This is where my cannabis smoking started again mixing with the other kids from around the way plus the kids that were there already known where to get it from so every Friday when we would get our pocket money from school and a few of us would chip in to buy beers, spirits, sweets, cigarettes, rizla papers, all the accessories we needed for that night and hit the park to get drunk & high. I wasn't that much of a drinker so a few sips of different liquor went straight to my head got tipsy very quickly plus the weed I pulled a good couple of "whities" where you feel like your going under and feels like something bad is about to happen it's not a good experience especially being young your heart rate goes up and starts racing dramatically feels like your going to die so if you ain't strong-minded it can overtake your thoughts an cause you to faint or worse suffer cardiac arrest.

There were programs set in place for certain individuals and because I got caught a few times they tried to put me on an alcohol awareness course which I refused because I thought that was a ridiculously undermining statement to make about me it was just an experiment mixing with the older guys having fun getting my first experience with girls.

My first time was completely lacklustre, it wasn't particularly special, and it certainly wasn't some great or life-changing event. If I can remember I was reaching the age of 12 years old and there was a girl I used to always see when I'd go to the shops down the road from home. So I can't really remember how or what happened but we ended speaking and she was asking questions about the home and why I was there she was very intrigued because she'd see me coming out the gates a few times and she said she's always wanted to know what was behind the walls of

Fairhaven. She lived not far from the home literally round the corner I recall her telling me to meet her outside one night that she had something to tell me which turned out that her parents were going away on holiday the upcoming weekend and she wanted me to come round I was excited and the following weekend I snuck out the window after roll count and went straight to her house. Emma she was called can't remember her last name but she was my first experience she was a few years older than me with a little more experience so she kind of schooled me a little bit it felt weird but nice because I didn't know what happened because my toes curled and I went stiff she explained that I had just popped my "cherry" in other words lost my virginity it was a crazy experience for my young self.

The next morning, I felt no different.

The prominence of the pain I felt lingered a bit, but it was nothing terrible.

There wasn't anything particularly memorable about the experience. It was, as I know now, pretty average. Below average, when it comes to my physical enjoyment of the experience now. It wasn't satisfying, but it did get the job done. I was no longer a virgin, and I was okay with it I was over the moon and proud of myself plus all the other kids were making fun of me because I was still a virgin so I felt good when I finally did it.

After a while of being at Fairhaven things strangely started to change for me like having my clothes stolen from my room when I'd be in the bathroom taking shower kids would rush in and take my clothes off the railing to leave me with no towel so I'd have to walk down the corridor to my room naked even my stuff started going missing from the room cd's, clothes, certain things that I'd notice would be missing. Things like that started to effectively fuck with my mind and because every one of the other kids was white at times I did feel like it was a racist attempt to bully me laugh and make fun out of me it was all psychological.

People often think of bullying as being physically violent towards another person, but bullying can take many forms – it can be physical, verbal, social or psychological. Bullying is repeated aggressive behaviour by a person or a group that is directed at another person or group and is intended to cause harm, distress or fear. Bullying could include making threats to someone, spreading rumours about them, attacking someone physically or verbally, or deliberately excluding someone from a group. Bullying doesn't just affect the person who is being bullied – it also has an impact on those who are witness to the bullying, as well as on those who bully.

Whatever form of bullying takes place, being bullied can have a huge impact on a young person's life, impacting their self-esteem and mental health. Sometimes someone may try to justify their behaviour by finding something different about the person they are bullying – this might include what they look like, how they express themselves or what they do. But this does not mean that the person being bullied is to blame.

There is never any justification for bullying.

Those silly games the other teenage kids were doing became relentlessly boring and frustrating for quite some time personally my anger was building up inside and I was a ticking time bomb waiting to explode. What ticked me off was one day I was walking down the corridor to my dorm and some kid stuck his foot out to trip me up it made my blood boil because other kids were laughing I wasn't having any of it I started fighting trying to stab the kid with this biro pen I had in my hand one of the windows In the hallway door smashed which alerted the staff who came rushing and split it up restrained us and was sent to our dormitory.

I'd sometimes have to meet a group of kids at the back of the home on the playing fields to have an arranged fight and like I said because I was the only mixed-race kid there it felt that I had to be extra tough and show the other kids I wasn't to be played with and certainly wasn't going to let them bully me.

Don't get me wrong I was sceptical and nervous because it was unknown what was going to happen and I used to think they'd jump me but I can say it was all one and one fights nobody jumped in there was an older kid there that took a liking to me and saw I wasn't a coward and wasn't just going to get bullied he prevented anything serious from happening to me he did have my back I'll never forget (Thomas) can't remember his second name but he wasn't actually in the home he lived around the area. That lasted for a good while where it seemed every week I'd have to fight even if at times I didn't want to I couldn't get made out to be a wimp so I had to stand my ground so in reality, it caught 22 for me because if I didn't fight they'd call me names and think that they could continuously belittle me and that would get me frustrated and mad so I'd end up fighting anyway so I was for sure going to gain my respect and earn a staunchly status.

There wasn't that much to entertain yourself with apart from listening to my favourite music that my sister Natalie sent in for me like 2pac & Master P and another rap artist what she knows I liked other than that you had to deal with what was provided in the establishment itself so we had to find amusement from somewhere. So one thing that I used to love doing with a few of the other kids was hiding behind the wall on the roof of the conservatory facing the road and throw pebble type stones at passing police cars they'd know it came from the residence at the home but couldn't identify which one of us was responsible for throwing the stones.

After a while, they put up a wooden board blocker so you couldn't access the roof of the conservatory so that eventually died down and was no longer something fun to do it was also our little smoking & drinking hideout as well you could stay up there for hours it was good in the winter too because you were covered by shelter it was a good little spot.

Fairhaven was more like a residential school more than a care home where you stayed through the week and went home on the weekends at this time it had been a good few years that I'd been in the system and in the hands of strangers making decisions on my behalf monopolising my whole life. I was going home more at this point but still had my bad days which lead to me not being able to go home because of my behaviour so it was still difficult and I was still trapped and my life was still being controlled and there was nothing I could do about it.

In my opinion, how I looked at being in that position back in the early 1990s is that (RESIDENTIAL/ BOARDING SCHOOLS) - Was built with two primary objectives and that was to remove and isolate children from the influence of their home, families, traditions and cultures, and to assimilate into the dominant culture. I witnessed many disturbing things at Fairhaven due to the mental health some kids suffered from plus receiving punishments was common at residential schools in the early 1990s with many students describing being assaulted in different ways and many students also experiencing sexual abuse.

One of the most devastating impacts of the residential school system was that it gave most students a poor education.

For many, that led to chronic unemployment or under-employment, poverty, poor housing, substance abuse, family violence, and ill-health. Even around the world Residential schools systematically undermined and disrupted families for generations, severing the ties through which different cultures are taught and sustained, and contributing to a general loss of language and their cultural beliefs.

I was only in Fairhaven for around 12 months before I was notified that I'd be moving to a school closer to home also my stay within the care system was due to end and the money was running low plus there was only so much they could do for me at Fairhaven because my circumstances were much different from the other kids my stay was more for the educational purposes plus challenging my behaviour. They did spend a lot of money on the kids at Fairhaven just like they did at the lower school they were always actively getting the kids involved in weekly activities like rock climbing, skating, ice skating, cinemas, discos, it was good in that way because you never boarded you always had things to do like play in the big games room play on the computers they had pool & snooker tables a duke box that had thousands of different types of music to choose from activity-wise despite it being the basics you made it fun. I eventually moved on from Fairhaven and was awaiting placement in another residential school but I had no idea where I was going next it kind of fucked with my mind not knowing the unknown but what could I do.

MISSING FOR A WEEK.

Before I was transferred from Fairhaven awaiting my placement in another care organisational environmental school.

I was placed in some house in Chester and my mum wasn't notified of that arranged move so she didn't know where I was for around a week. I remember phoning my mum and she was asking where I was and I told her I'd been moved from Fairhaven to some other house in Chester. She asked to speak to the people responsible for looking after me which was two middle-aged couples and it was just me living there nobody else it was an old creepy house and I didn't like it I felt there was something funny about the house and the couple. I can't remember too much as my memory for that period is a bit blurry because I didn't stay there for that long but I remember the woman always coming into my room saying weird stuff to me sitting on the bottom of my bed with her hand on my leg like she's making sure I'm ok as a mother would do the type of thing but it was a completely different feeling she was weird. Plus at that time I was kind of worried because I was thinking for 1. what type of decisions was being made and who within the care system would not notify my mum of any changes regarding her son. That made me a bit more resentful of the system and I didn't last long maybe 2 weeks max but I think it was a temporary accommodation while I was waiting to go to my next unknown destination. I started shoplifting cd's from H.M.V and running out of shops with sweets anything I wanted I would take It's like I didn't know the meaning of paying for stuff I'd just take it and run off. I got arrested a lot and cautioned for many different reasons at that stage my record was building up to more serious crimes which were noticeable from the authorities. The house in Chester was temporary accommodation until a handwritten letter was given to me explaining I'd be moving to arrow park hall Merseyside.

ARROW HALL.

The early history of Arrow Park is entwined with the Shaw family. Arrow Hall was built in 1835 by John Ralph Shaw on the site of a smaller building, Arrow House. It was enlarged over the next fifty years, the imposing entrance hall being added in 1880. He furnished it with 'mock- Elizabethan' furniture, some of which can be seen on display at the Williamson Art Gallery and Museum in Birkenhead.

John Shaw had purchased the first piece of land which lies within the present park boundaries. The 'Mayor of Liverpool' twice (in 1794 and 1800), he was not well-liked by his peers, who thought him foolish for caring for the poor and needy during his term of office. He held very few receptions and gave what monies would have been spent to charity. A wealthy shipowner, John Shaw allowed his ships to transport 'slaves' from Africa to America. At the time though, this was seen by many people as being a decent profession. John Ralph (Nicholson) Shaw was a great-nephew of John Shaw. To inherit the estate of his great-uncle, he had to change his name from Nicholson to Shaw. John Ralph Shaw was responsible for most of the landscaping of the park, much of which remains unchanged today. He constructed the lake and waterfall on the estate by damming and changing the direction of the Arrowebrook. In 1837, he married Fanny Cruttenden, a vicar's daughter from Alderley and they had 12 children.

John Ralph Shaw was a magistrate and was very hard on any trespassers or poachers who were brought before him. On the Estate at Arrowe, to ensure people did not stray from the public footpath that crossed his lands, he installed 'mantraps' and 'spring-loaded shotguns'. His daughters played a strong role in Woodchurch CE School, helping teach singing and needlework. John Ralph Shaw would also open the estate for the school to hold picnics for the children.

William Otto Nicholson Shaw succeeded his father in 1884. He was an Oxford student, where he gained a BA, and went on to become a Major in the Cheshire Yeoman Cavalry.

The family graves of the Shaw family can be found in the churchyard at Holy Cross, Woodchurch.

At the turn of the century, Arrowe Estate became the property of a Major McCalmont, but as he was serving with the army he leased it to Mr Williamson ('Williamson Art Gallery, Birkenhead'), a Liverpool shipping magnate.

The Williamsons left for Allerton Towers (in Liverpool) and in 1917 the estate passed to Lord Leverhulme, who let it to the Johnson family.

In 1926 the estate was purchased by Birkenhead Corporation on the understanding that it was to be used for the people of the borough.

In 1929 the World Scout Jamboree was held in the park, which was a great success despite the rain! Following the Jamboree the first playground was built, including swings, seesaws and maypoles.

During the 1930s the golf course was laid out, along with bowling greens and tennis courts. The public used to flock to the hall on summer weekends to listen to brass bands playing on the lawn, while part of the hall was used as a café.

At the start of the Second World War, the Hall became a headquarters for the army. After being rescued from Dunkerque many French soldiers were billeted in huts on the estate. Senegalese soldiers who were part of the Free French Army were accommodated on the estate, while their officers lived at the Hall.

The park was also used as a tank training area, it is not true that the strange 'corrugations' on parts of the golf course and woodland (for example 16th. and 17th. fairways) were caused by the tanks (nor are they remnants of a medieval field system). They emanate from Ralph Shaw's tree planting, allowing thousands of seedlings to be 'grown on' while the shallow trenches acted as a drainage channel to save the roots rotting from excess water.

As can be seen on other website photographs, golf continued throughout the war despite the tanks and the course returned to full use after the war and is considered a good challenge, being used as a qualifying course for the Open.

The Hall has been used as a convalescent home for the Birkenhead hospitals and later became a respite weekend home for disabled children.

The recent history of the hall has been riddled with uncertainty. While it had been left to decline, the hall has been cleaned and is now looking beautiful again. An American bid was put in for the Hall to become a 'Teddy Bear Factory', but it was rumoured that this was a cover to take over the golf course and privatise it, the hall to become a hotel.

This faded when it was apparent that the golf course could not be sold. Wirral Ranger Service has shown little interest in taking charge of the Hall as its offices and a viability study by the Golf Club showed that it would be uneconomic to adopt the Hall as a clubhouse. The hall is currently being utilised as a private respite and care home for children. That place was spooky I have to say I didn't like that place like a big mansion house massive too big for me and a few other kids that were living there at that time with me. I was there for a few months if I can remember my stay there wasn't that memorable but I know it was just another establishment where I had to be out of my control. I was sent from there to a more mainstream type boarding school called Clarence House.

CLARENCE HOUSE SCHOOL.

Clarence High School provides both Residential and day Placements in a therapeutic setting for both boys and girls who experience social, emotional and behavioural difficulties who may also experience more complex difficulties, including those on the autistic spectrum.

Nugent Care is a charitable organisation that offers a diverse range of support to adults and children across Liverpool and throughout the North West of England.

The origins of Nugent Care date back to the 1800s and the pioneering work of Father James Nugent (1822-1905) concerning child welfare, relief from poverty and social reform.

The work of Father Nugent had a dramatic impact on the lives of thousands of vulnerable people and his work continues to this day through Nugent Care.

I used to get a taxi which was organised by the school every week from home back to Clarence House school with a girl who started round about the time as I called Kirsty Anstee same age as me and lived in the Trafford area of Stretford a few miles from where I lived.

The taxi driver would drop us off every Friday afternoon and come and collect us on a Sunday evening ready to start school the following morning on Monday and that would be our routine every week for months and until we left or things changed.

Kirsty was a hard blazer just like myself so every Sunday afternoon on the way back to Clarence House we would get the taxi driver Jeff to stop off at the shop get bare munchies for the journey and for when we got back to our destination.

Jeff was a cool taxi driver he used to let us smoke in his taxi that's after me always antagonising him to let us smoke so in the end he gave up he was one of those guys that told you stories about back in the day and said he was a bit like us in his younger days I have to say he was a cool guy used to tell me I smell like an Amsterdam coffee shop (Haha). Soon as we got back we'd sign in at the office put our belongings in our rooms then hit the posh formby evening streets to blaze leaving a trail of that good aroma in the air for people to inhale as their walking past people looking at us walking down the street thinking we're crazy and they knew we came from the school but we didn't care Kirsty would just throw the middle finger up laugh at them and we would keep it stepping.

One thing that used to piss us off though was when we had appointments to go opticians or doctors and they would bring us in this big blue minibus with disabled signs and logos representing that we ain't normal kids and the looks we used to get from people like we were different humans was annoying but it did look like a bus that was used to carry the insane I used to hate sitting on that bus I think we all did. Kirsty was small around 5 foot 1 petite with glasses plus she was pretty looked like she was too innocent to be there but she did have a wild temper she wasn't shy at all, most of the girls and boys that was there at the school whether they stayed through the week or came from the outside of Birkenhead but the majority of them were from Liverpool so you can imagine 20 years ago being in a school especially not a normal school in Liverpool when you're from Manchester it's not going to be that easy and believe me it wasn't easy for the both of us but we had to stick together and I always had her back no matter what.

I remember two scouse girls were living in the house that we stayed in through the week Natalie & Zoe there names were and these girls would always harass Kirsty bully her try to get her to do stuff call her names make fun out of her always tormenting her to the point where I had to intervene a few times because I don't like bullies no matter what species they could be woman or man I despise it especially coming from Fairhaven where I was getting the same similar treatment an I could see this happening over time to Kirsty but at that time I was fucking Natalie so I told her to leave her alone stop bullying. This kept happening under my nose so one day Kirsty came to me and said:

KIRSTY- I want to fight them both but I know they're going to jump me so can you distract Natalie while I go beat up Zoe.

I was amazed and felt her frustration because she had been going through this for quite some time and I don't know what ticked her off that day but she was ready and don't get me wrong small and looked like she wouldn't hurt a fly but deep down she was a feisty one when she was ready it just needed something to bring that out well on this day it came out she was ready plus I'd never seen her so riled up.

We orchestrated a plan to separate Natalie & Zoe so I called Natalie into the room with me to give me a B.J while Kirsty ran up on Zoe in her room and went to work on her as a human punch bag and I had to give it to Kirsty though because Zoe wasn't small either she had a bit of weight behind her a lot stronger than Kirsty but Kirsty had more heart and that's what came out on top at the end. After around 15 20 minutes or soo I came out to see Zoe's ginger hair all scruffy cut lip scratches all over her face she looked tired as well breathing heavy sure she was even crying cheeks all red and puffed up she looked a mess. Natalie found out what had happened to her mate and wanted to get her revenge so a few days had passed and Kirsty and Natalie had a fight but Kirsty won Natalie or Zoe could not fight and they didn't even have the heart like Kirsty they were just hard when they were together, in the end, I was proud of Kirsty for standing up for herself and she never got bullied again she was cool.

I used to exchange weed for weed but different types with the lads from Liverpool there was one kid who always brought weed into a school called "JACKO" he had the Polly a weed which is very popular that they have in Liverpool and I had skunk a weed that was popular in Manchester also known as (SKIZZA).

Every day without fail I'd be in the class in school and my eyes would be so red I'd look like the devil it was obvious that I was blazing, the teachers reporting me because they say I'm smelling of cannabis it got to the point where they would search my stuff on arrival when I got back from a weekend at home they were on me hard. Plus I was a menace in the school itself and I found myself always in the (isolation room) stuck there for hours hungry and the worst part about it is you'll always miss out on your dinner and get sandwiches and a pack of chicken or mushroom soup and you've probably only had the lunch which gets provided by the home everybody else who comes from outside goes to the shop at lunchtime or has the school prepared meal. After the week the school would have an appointment in the hall which everyone would have to attend. Here is where they calculate a point system for each class and award students with winning activities for their learning and attendance and that can consist of getting tickets for the cinema getting to go on the quad bikes all sorts of different types of awards you could get but me Kirsty and rest our class never got shit we were a low class the dead Beat class with all the tare aways the bad kids who didn't listen and wanted to do there own stuff don't think we ever got awarded anything, to be honest, we were just ruthlessly doing our shit.

We did have a lot of fun there though when I think we had funny moments and we also had some dark moments but we kept each other sane plus because I and Kirsty were the only Mancunian people there we felt we have to stick together more anyways plus I didn't like bullies so that brought us closer together me protecting her and she felt that she knew I wouldn't sell her down the river in times of need because I proved that on multiple occasions.

A few funny things stand out for me that we had to do when we wanted to chill especially at night because the girls and boys could mix but they couldn't be in the same room together with the door closed that was a rule but we didn't listen to that shit. I used to climb out my front bedroom window run round to the back to get to Kirsty's window throw a stone and smoke chat to her way that's until I came up with a plan to distract the night clocker who was on night shift. I used to put pillows in my bed to look like I was sleeping sneak out along the side of the corridor because the night clocker used to sit right outside in the hallway so he could see people coming in and out of their dorms but I was slick plus a bit assistance from being under the darkness as the lights would be off I'd sneak all the way around till I get to Kirsty's room tap on the door 3 times which was our little code and we would be chilling all night hanging out the window blazing chatting to each other about life until the light broke through the curtains but I had to hide when the night clocker was done there rounds every hour or so thinking back we were only twelve years old minors but seen and been through so much already at that time. Because of my constant bad behaviour and all the smoking weed in school coming in smelling of cannabis disrespecting the teachers not listening in class fighting the funds they had from social was seemingly becoming a waste of money because I was not taking anything seriously especially after what I've had to deal with being that age already they terminated my stay and excluded me. To my knowledge and from doing my research I believe Clarence House after so many years is finally due to close its doors due to close due to financial difficulties R.I.P Clarence House.

EDGERTON HIGH SCHOOL

After I was excluded from Clarence House I went to a few more schools for challenging youths in the Manchester Trafford areas like Flixton, Timperley, Urmston, and Stretford I didn't last long at any of those establishments as I remember getting arrested for beating up the headmaster strangled him with his tie and threw a chair at his head. That day they blagged me told me that they had phoned my mum and she was on the way to collect me Little did I know they had phoned the police and when I thought it was my mum outside waiting for me it was the police I made off assaulting the policeman and pushing my way past them. I made it home that day from Timperley but was arrested the following morning for assault on a police officer and G.B.H on the headteacher.

Edgerton high was one of the last schools I want to actually before officially coming out the care system was the old Edgerton Road high school before they built the new at this stage I'm more living at home at the age of 14 and Edgerton Road high school was the last resort there was nowhere else for me to go no other mainstream schools would take me it was the end of the line after all I've just had a long spell through the care system and the record shows I'm a handful and be a handful in every school I've ever been too.

My friend AARON ORR aka (DRAG ZINO) lived around the corner from one another very good and loyal friend of mine we went to the same school Edgerton Road High he was always a witness to my madness and thought I was a little lunatic especially because we knew each other from the hood so he knew exactly what I was like.

I was always on the roof throwing slated tiles off smashing windows police would be called a dozen times a week I'd see the van pulling up in the car park and if the teachers trying to lock me in I'd be out the windows getting chased out of school wondering the streets at school time wanted by police.

I remember flooding the whole building all the corridors were soaked the school had to be evacuated because of electrical problems I terrorised the place causing thousands of pounds worth of criminal damage, I reached the age of 15 whilst still going to Edgerton Road High school and was excluded for causing the flood plus bringing weed into school together with my behaviour that they couldn't manage or control.

The teachers kept telling me this is the last stop for you the next stop is prison cells, I laughed probably gave the middle finger and continued to do badness I was individually like that as well so there was no pressure or following friends most of my friend's parents didn't want there kids playing with me because they said I was a bad influence so I hardly had anyone that was doing what I was doing apart from a handful like (Jamie Fitzgerald) (Antwon Elson) (Scott Street)(Thomas Cartwright) (Zico Reid) (Micha Stewart) (Errol Junior) and a few more but they were all close to me growing up and had an impact in my life in some way we were all from different worlds but the same type of mentality so we were relatable had things in common.

Before I commence onto the next chapter I would just like to say thank you to everyone reading my book I appreciate you taking the time out to read my story understanding my life before passing judgment also I appreciate you respecting my beliefs and seeing things through the eyes of mine as you travel through my life with me.

I am recognising I am only human at the end of the day who does make mistakes and I hope it gives the younger generations who may be reading these certain things to think about and gives you lessons from my experiences that could lead you to make better choices & decisions in your life.

I don't regret not getting a good education because like I said through the most part I've educated myself and had to have an understanding of the world we live in at a very early age a lot younger than most children so through my knowledge of experiences I hope to target not only the children but adults as well.

After all, you can never know too much and everybody has a story to tell plus it's good to connect your brains to different frequencies to allow your knowledge to grow in other words, be around good people those that wish nothing but the best for your health & wealth honourable loyal & respectable staunch people.

Crime doesn't pay and it certainly cost too much to be a criminal.

Think about your life try to stay away from drugs and alcohol especially in an uncontrolled environment.

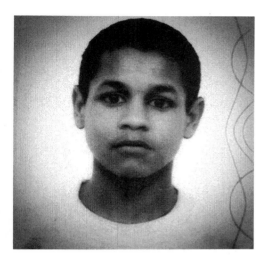

Aaron, aged 9 whilst in care

Aaron, 11 years old

CHAPTER SIX

The Streetz.
They Don't Love You.

Growing up one thing that I witnessed that did affect me as a 7-year-old boy was a big group fight with the "blacks" & "Somalians" right outside my house on the walking path. I don't think it was fair to be honest because from what I could see there was only 3 Somalians and they had about 5-6 black guys on them and I mean they were big men not small either but to me they all looked like giants and all I could see was these boots and trainers jumping on the heads of these Somalians I remember my mum coming out because she could hear all the shouting and commotion from inside saw what was happening and shouted at me to get away & get inside. After all, I found myself edging closer & closer very intrigued about this brawl. Not even half-hour had passed maybe say ten-fifteen minutes before ambulances & blue siren lights were at the scene all I kept thinking was it didn't end well for those other guys because from what I could see is that they was in a bad way, not something I wanted to witness but I couldn't help it I was intrigued.

My mums' bedroom window was facing the front where I could see what was happening to hear all the sirens and seeing the flashing blue lights it was like a movie scene to a young man and that's something I was seeing regularly growing up in an unstable environment it's inevitable that you may be exposed to violence it's just the way it is and the way the is was you can't control it.

There were many things that I saw just going to the shops with my mum police chases, cars speeding past with blue lights flashing serious car crashes with dead bodies in them that I've seen right in front of my eyes shit that's real shit that's not normal the effect that it can have on a child is detrimental to the brain even down to the movies we watch most of it is all learnt behaviour.

They say the eyes are the window to the soul and we shouldn't leave any bad undesirable traces of negativity for others to follow especially as a child.

Through the eyes of mine growing up, I had a lot of influences around me that probably unconsciously shaped my life to what it was going to be.

The negativity affected the way I looked and saw certain things in the world we live in because if I wasn't so interested in being on the street maybe my interests would off been in something else that was more positive like the love for music I have or the love for certain sports etc.

I had a problem with authority from an early age and especially after Trevor past I was on the wrong side of the law by then already. Age 6 is when I started being on the streets and doing badness and always exploring the neighbourhood for myself seeing things I shouldn't have been exposed to but it's all part of the growth as a child some children are born into a different environment a good neighbourhood and there are kids like myself that unfortunately didn't have that luxury.

Because I was so eager to be outside I found myself constantly up to no good and with watching older guys I started to understand the streets more and before I knew it I was drawn into the dark side of life where the criminals, killers, drug dealers, car thieves, burglars were and once that happened it was very difficult for me to ignore the temptations of the street life.

Many films that I saw growing up maybe shouldn't off been on display for me to watch because they caught my attention for all sorts reasons, I'd stay at a friends house and their older brothers would have stacks of CD's or films containing criminal explicit behaviour and we'd watch them also learning along the way I can name a few like In the 1991 film,

New Jack City, the character Nino Brown played by (Wesley Snipes) and his associates, were largely based on the Chambers Brothers.

As in the movie, the Chambers Brothers were also known for taking over an apartment complex known as The Broadmoor on E.

Movies like CB4 a 1993 American comedy film directed by Tamra Davis and starring comedian Chris Rock. The film follows a fictional rap group named "CB4", named after the prison block in which the group was allegedly formed (Cell Block 4).

(Clockers the movie) this plot and story stood out for me as a young man about Nineteen-year-old "Strike" Dunham (Mekhi Phifer) is a small-time street drug dealer for Rodney Little (Delroy Lindo), who wants Strike to kill a former dealer who stole from him. When the man turns up dead, Strike is suspected. But before homicide detective Rocco Klein (Harvey Keitel) has a chance to investigate, Strike's brother, Victor (Isaiah Washington), confesses to the crime – and Klein suspects that Victor, a virtuous family man, is trying to cover up for Strike.

To mention a good few ghetto hood movies that I was exposed to growing up I'd have to go into the archives to give you an insight into how watching these films on VHS at an early age would off and most definitely impaired my thoughts and had me thinking differently.

Plus there was a lot of musical influences that were around at that time old school rap that real hip hop sound plus I remember me and my very good friend (Zico

"C-Loc" Reid) who I've grown with since knee-high was always listening to some shit that was street or gang-related I even remember we recorded the album (The Last Don, Master P) of the Tim Westwood radio 1 rap show back in the late 1990s around 1999. My movies and CD's list of the 90's early '00s;>.

To the present day. Friday, 1995

- New Jersey Drive, 1995
- La Haine, 1995
- Don't be a menace to south central whilst drinking your juice in the hood, 1996
- Sunset Park, 1996
- Original gangstas, 1996
- Bullet, 1996
- Set it off, 1996
- The substitute, 1996
- I'm bout it, 1997
- One Eight Seven, 1997
- Ma 6-T va crack-er, 1997
- Squeeze, 1997
- First-time felon, 1997
- Always outnumbered, 1998
- He got game, 1998
- Streetwise, 1998
- Da game of life, 1998
- I got the hookup, 1998

- Caught up, 1998
- Belly, 1998
- Slam, 1998
- In too deep, 1999
- Colorz of rage, 1999
- Urban menace, 1999
- Light it up, 1999
- Hot boys, 1999
- White boyz, 1999

Artist & music influences.

- Brother lynch hung
- Aceyalone
- Atmosphere
- No Limit
- Black star
- Blackalicious
- X-Raided
- Wu Tan Clang
- Dilated peoples
- Seagram
- Hieroglyphics
- J-Live
- Juggaknots
- Dmx
- Latyrx

- Loot pack
- LL Cool J
- Slum village
- The coup
- Three six mafia
- BlackJack
- The Pharcyde
- Run D MC

That's on some real-life shit, most films and music that I took a liking to and was exposed to was based around true life experiences that I liked to see & hear so I could get an understanding of the pictures they were painting through words & rhyme. Some were fictional and some weren't but it still had that criminal influence on how I thought things were supposed to be in society and the world. Even music played a big part in my young life because I got taught to understand by one of my closest friends at the time called Adam.

He lived just down the street on the corner of Birchlane he was a lot older than me by a good few years and we become friends as well as a lot of other kids by kicking the ball on the street and playing water fights in the summer, my next-door neighbour Bradley Benjamin knew him first and then we just kind of congregated and became good friends growing up together on the same street.

Adams favourite rap artist back then was (Snoop Dogg) the Doggy Style album which was released in 1993 but it was the late 1990's when my eardrums first heard that underground rap sound.

So you can see from a very young age I've been exposed to certain things both in real life and through the TV.

Violence and crime became reality for me not just watching it through the T.V so it didn't seem too daunting seeing violence and crime because It became the norm like watching a scary movie it was more exciting and curious to the unknown.

One of the movies that I found interesting and thought were real-life robots was Terminator 2: Judgment Day made in (1991).

I first watched it around 1994-1995 and I find it's the best action sci-fi flick movie from the 90's ever made and I would strongly say it's one of the greatest of all time in my opinion.

Terminator 2 is my favourite film I love this movie to death! It's my number 1 best movie ever till today the best of the best epic movie of all time. T2 was nominated for 4.

It made me think about (Skynet) and computers and the dynamics of the world of telecommunications and the stuff that might be hidden from us because films don't get made for nothing without a hidden message within them, it was just my way of thinking I wasn't one to disregard my feelings I took as knowledge even as a young man.

Seeing the terminator and all the robots was fascinating, I was hooked I used to watch it 2-3 times a day without fail I couldn't get enough of the film I loved it it's what made me have a taste for firearms as well as seeing warren for the first time at the age of six years old shoot his pistol through a cushion.

I remember climbing on some rooftops one day messing around and ended up in the back of some laundrette on Dickinson Road Longsight just a few hundred yards from my house, as I was throwing stuff over the wall into the alleyway I kicked this black bin bag full of clothes and under the bags was a brown 177 calibre air rifle,

I stashed it in some old building around the corner from my house and used to practice shooting cans and bottles of the wall every day until I lost it splitting my head open in the empty old house on nails stuck in wood trying to locate the rifle.

As a kid I was always reluctant to go to bed; wanting to stay up late because I always thought that I was missing out on something always intrigued about things adventurous way too eager I couldn't keep still it was like I had ants in my pants curious about the unknown.

Being adventurous means you're willing to go where you haven't been before and do things you've never done, even if you don't know how it's going to turn out and that's basically how I looked at things.

My mum knew how intrigued I was as a young kid because she caught me a few times trying to reenact the actions out of the classic children's film (Home Alone) outside my house trying to trip people up with some homemade traps or making slingshots to shoot people with that was just start of many things to come.

Explicit TV programs would come on and my mum would say it's time for bed because it's something she watches and it wouldn't be suitable for young people to view but I always wanted to stay up.

I'm talking about programmes like (Band of Gold) which were a British television crime drama series, written and created by Kay Mellor, that was the first broadcast on ITV on 12 March 1995. Produced by Granada Television, the series revolves around the lives of a group of sex workers who live and work in Bradford's red-light district.

I would blag my mum that I'm going upstairs and sneak back in and hide behind the sofa behind her; she'd notice me then send me to bed I would have been between 7-8 years old thinking back to 1995 when It was first published.

But it's program's like that plus all the other movies that affect a child's mind and it's understandable now looking back that my mum didn't want me to watch something so explicit & graphic as (Band of Gold) or gangster shit where you see people getting shot and killed women getting murdered & raped, drugs, alcoholics, police, criminals etc it's not good for the mind as it's powerful messages can influence the innocence of the youth.

I started my criminal behaviour from the age of five very much while still in school as I explained in the chapter of my time in education, I won't say it was because of the films or the tv programs I was watching or the music I was listening too, It's more to do with wanting to explore the world for myself and discover what write & wrong is when in it came to do things that are required "criminal".

Plus it was more realistic for me to see what others were doing out on the street, I didn't need to watch films to see violence it was practically on my doorstep every time I'd go shop or just be out playing It wasn't long before I'd see a police chase or see a section of the area cornered and taped off by police because someone's just been shot or stabbed.

To see things like that at a very early age in my opinion does affect the way you are as an individual because at five-six years old your innocence is pure there are not many things in life to worry about; life is good for most at that age, but on the flip side where you grow up plays a big part of your character because we live through seeing traumatic events that can have a big impact on a child's life also having to defend yourself from trouble makers or worse robbed for your stuff.

I can think of a few times that may have caused my attitude towards society to be rebellious against all adults especially authority, one being as a child 6-7 years old skateboarding with my neighbours' poodle (fluffy) through Platt fields park when I was approached by a young mixed-race male around 14 too 15 years old.

He didn't say a word to me and I certainly didn't think he was going to do anything when all of sudden I just felt these hands in my chest like a big thud knocking me over off the skateboard as I fell my hands scraped on the concrete to prevent my face & head smashing on the ground (fluffy) got scared and ran off still attached to the lead and the guy just took off with my skateboard. I wasn't exactly crying but I was upset and angry that I've just been robbed for my skateboard not only that I've just lost (fluffy) the neighbours poodle, I searched and searched the perimeter of the park until it was getting a little dark plus I know I had to be back home and sue ain't going to be best pleased to hear that (fluffy) has run away and I've not been able to find her.

I got home and explained to my mum that I've just had my skateboard took and (fluffy) the dog had run off and she ain't come back, my mum took me round to Sue's and explained about what had just happened in the park.

To be honest; Sue was more concerned about my well-being and if I was okay she was a lovely woman old aged woman who lived on the corner just a few hundred yards away from my house.

She called the police to report (fluffy) missing but I couldn't tell the police anything apart from the information they already knew from Sue that my skateboard got took and (fluffy) ran away, at the same time I wasn't interested in reporting my skateboard or the robber I was irately angry inside thinking of the guys face wanting to get revenge and kill the bastard. Another time being the same age probably a year older walking through my estate again approached this time by an older black male who must've been in his late teens asked me where I was going and where I was from, I didn't understand what he was saying until he grabbed me and started pushing up against the wall that was behind me. It was around the New Year of 1997 Christmas time and my mum had bought me a digital Casio watch for Christmas and this prick snapped it off my wrist and ran off down the street.

That one really mentality damaged me as a young man because even though I was a bad kid and done things myself, I'd never had have the thought of robbing a young kid younger than me I was just adventurous who liked to explore far as I went for the crime was a little bit of criminal damage but not robbing people I was only 8 years old I still had a little bit of innocence within me despite my faults.

Those two occasions as a young boy affected me because as I got older It made me more viscous on the streets and not want to respect others for their shit, I was only young and I'd already been robbed twice and the thought of (fluffy) running away scared because some guy wants to bully a child and steel his skateboard I carried those faces in my mind for years even until this day 20+ years later they've stayed with me like a permanent scar.

(WARREN CURLEY.)

I remember one day being at my aunties boyfriends flat Warren, I must be about 6–7 years old at the time and I remember him going out of the room for a good few minutes think he went to do something outside and me not being able to keep still messing around like I had ants in my pants started kicking some type of fitness ball around the living room. I kicked the ball and an ornament which was on the cabinet fell off the side & smashed into a thousand pieces on the floor, I realised I'd fucked up and tried to clean it up as quick as possible but to make matters worse I could hear Warren coming back in so I didn't have enough time and started thinking shit and just covered it with a black duffel type bag that was next to the sofa.

Unknown to me as he came back in I didn't clean the floor properly so little bits of the small broken glass was still on the floor as he came in he stomps on the crushed little bits making a crunching sound he looks down and sees all these shattered bits of glass all over the floor. Immediately looks at me as if to say what the fuck is this I just look at him and say "sorry" in a little voice he smiles & laughs and replies "don't worry about it" there's no need to cry over spilt milk.

Even though I was young I was understanding for a young man and I was smart enough to realise that when people are doing dodgy shit and Warren saw that in me so he wanted to teach me as well guide me with knowledge so he never hid anything from me he educated and wanted me to learn regardless of what it was.

Growing up there's something that I've nothing mentioned to anyone ever before until now, especially because my auntie Caroline or my mum wouldn't have been best pleased to hear me being around any criminal activity especially firearms at a young age but this was reality for me it's what I've seen and been exposed to hence the title;

(Through The Eyes Of Mine).

He grabbed the black bag and said to me don't tell your auntie or mum they'll kill me if they find out, I was so excited like a kid in a sweet shop waiting to see what he was gonna show me. He reached inside the black duffle type bag pulled out a small black hand pistol my eyes lit up I was amazed because I'd never seen a real gun before apart from the cap guns my mum used to get me from the paper shop or watching some gangster movies.

He tested it in the cupboard against a cushion "BANG" a semi loud bang muffled through the small living room with a small echo breaching my ears.

I started giggling and asked him can I have a go "No" he responded this ain't for kids and whatever you do "don't tell your mum" she'll kill me.

But what I'm going to do is show you how to handle it how you would use it I couldn't believe it he dismantled it and put it back together like a professional marksman he must have had a lot of experience because nobody accomplishes that without knowing what there doing thinking back he did come from Dublin Ireland so it probably explains why he was so smooth with it.

My lips have been sealed for over 20+ years but it's about time I let that shit out because at end of the day it's been my life experience and regardless of who may think "negatively" about it, it's a specific moment I'll cherish because it did become very helpful knowledge not just for me but for others too later on in life.

Warren was no ordinary civilian he was more M.O.B (MAN OF BIZNIZ).

He was involved in many things & one thing I do remember he used to ring cars clone them and ship them back to Dublin Ireland he also used to clone vehicles do armed robberies to avoid capture he was a smooth criminal because I don't think he ever got arrested maybe the police knew about his character but he was intelligent enough to avoid capture that's all that matters. I never really knew that side to him until that first time I saw a real pistol but he has only ever shown that side when it was just me and him together he has never done anything when my sister was around he kept that separate for reasons I don't know why I can only think he probably didn't want to expose a girl to that life or for her to see that side to him thinking about it it's understandable.

I vaguely remember him saying to me that there was a group of Irish mobsters looking for him so I think that's the reason he armed himself with a gun because his life was at risk for something he'd done back home in Dublin Ireland and they knew he was in England so I guess he had mixed emotions also probably paranoid and wanted to protect his life by any means necessary.

Warren was always into some shit in the mix of something criminality might as well of be his second name despite him being involved in crime or how he lived his life he never once initiated me to do anything criminal always gave me good advice and told me to get an education also have respect be good for my mum but through the eyes of mine I was already influenced I think it was just too late you couldn't undo the things I'd already had seen I had the respect I was just more cheeky and mis-chievous.

Due to moving from where we were at the time plus him & my auntie Caroline splitting up the last time I heard off Warren or heard anything about him was in the early 1990s. I recall my auntie Caroline informing me that he had been beaten up because he cloned a vehicle in which he has also done a robbery in and it didn't quite turn out so well for him. Something to do with the guys' registration plate who he cloned got arrested and was a suspect for the robbery of cash and transit so the police thought it was them because the same registration had been reported in the robbery to the police.

What a position for him to be in unknown to him driving the cloned vehicle with the same number plate the guys in the other car recognised the plate and gave chase wrote him off the road and made mincemeat out off him put him in hospital she told me they supposed to of really went to work on him nearly killing him I'm sure he was in a coma for a few weeks or so but pulled through.

That was around 1995-1996 and I think after that hap-pened to him and all the other shit he was involved in I think his stay in England was coming to an end I heard he flew the nest back to Dublin Ireland and was never to be seen or heard of again.

So a message to (Warren Curley) if you ever by any chance stumble across my autobiography just know that your missed and I've always had you in my thoughts and I hope you are in good health and spirit may our spiritual frequencies forever be locked together you'll forever be in my heart.

MANDY & THE PUNTERS.

Like many of the patrons after a few too many on a Saturday night, Tib Street is named after one of Manchester's 'lost rivers. A stream connecting to the River Medlock that ran through to Castlefield from Miles Platting in the 1700s came past what is now Oldham Road.

The pathway running beside it is our beloved Tib Street. Due to frequent flooding, the path had to be 'culverted' – meaning the stream now runs completely underground.

Each time Mandy got into a stranger's car, or was working the streets of Manchester's red-light districts she ran the risk of robbery and violent attack.... and, four, five maybe 6 times a week she would be on the front line showing off her long legs in a tight red skirt with her brown unkempt hair & black creased leather jacket with star shapes as patterns on it, her zip was broke and the high heels she wore I could tell was hurting her feet. Mandy was ruthless but on the other hand a lost soul with a caring and warm heart that sadly turned cold due to drugs and the life she was subjected to being abused by past relationships and a volatile upbringing as a child not having a steady life like many others. I met Mandy with my homeboy (Scott Street) when we used to be in the town centre late at night robbing and sneaking into buildings & restaurants to steel liquor, food, cash, and most things we could sell to the black market whether they were the Chinese, Asians, polish, whites, blacks, it could've been anyone we had a brain for making money young hustlers not scared ready for whatever. One day I remember being grounded by my mum because a few days before the police came to question me for criminal damage on somebody's property where I smashed the windows on some man's car because he caught me on his roof so I was grounded, grounding me never worked as my mum used to hide my trainers.

After all, it wouldn't be long before I was out the back bedroom window and out into the wilderness wandering the murky streets of Manchester.

This one particular day though I couldn't find my trainers so my sister had some unisex Nike air max so I threw them on and out the window I was into the darkness of the Mancunian street's, I was living in Old Trafford at the time on Beever Street I was around 9 years old and I remember meeting my friend Scott street in the (HUT) a shelter that he was always in because he was homeless himself and had a rough upbringing no mum no dad no family he was a survivor a grafter and I took a liking to him because I felt his pain and understood him we could relate in many ways I met Scott through my other mate that I grew up with called (Antwon Elson) he's another good friend he also has an older brother called Wesley both of them was on the same type of shit with us growing up always into some shit with the authorities. The (HUT) was near the red light district where all the prostitution took place most of the drug-taking & selling plus a lot of muggings and assaults happened here as well residents were scared off passing through especially at midnight hours the red light district was the dark side of life on the streets of Manchester that not many people my age got to see this place was not for the faint-hearted you had to be streetwise otherwise it wouldn't be long before you'd fall victim to the hands of a demon lurking the rat-infested alleyways.

This is where we met Mandy working the strip, it was like it was her occupation to be out there morning noon & night being the entertainment for the horny men driving up & down the strip in their flashy cars with semi-hard dicks half of them that she encounters with are probably married with wife's & good lives but looking a quick dirty £20 fuck after a long days shift at work.

Scott was older than me by a good few years so he was more streetwise when it came to doing certain things and how you should move and go about things, I can say he taught me how to be more stealth instead of being loud and blatant because I didn't care I would just take shit in front of people but that brought attention & many chases by police so it was about doing things quietly so the eyes can't see because he did teach me that the hand is quicker than the eye if you do it in the right way.

One of the main sources of income what we used to do was steal most of the liquor from the back of the restaurants and sell them to different people, shops, other restaurants, people on the street, crates of different wines and spirits stashed all over town some would get taken but they'll be some we couldn't even get rid off so we'd just have to leave them, in other words, we'd bite off more then we could chew at times so it taught me a very valuable lesson also that being hungry & greedy ain't always plausible you can end up losing out more then what you think your gonna make but on the flip side to that (it is NOT WHAT YOU KNOW, ITS WHO YOU KNOW) in that criminal life.

Scott knew this guy that used to be around near the (HUT) called Jammy Sammy the name was given to him because he just found a way to convince people to buy stolen stuff because we were too young people didn't take us seriously and a few times we did get robbed at knifepoint by other grafters it was scary at times but I had a brave heart I had too anyway especially "me" because I was tiny plus 26 years ago a little black boy getting around town just looked suspicious for people to see not even accompanied by an adult it just didn't look right even me would look and think what's he up to.

Mandy came into the picture ironically because of Jammy Sammy really, and it was jammy Sammy who introduced Mandy to me and Scott one night when we were patrolling the streets of the town centre looking for something to rob bored causing antisocial behaviour.

Jammy Sammy drove some white Volkswagen Polo S reg that had dints and some scratches in the bodywork but still looked clean at the same time because the rims he had on it made it stand out like a little sports car it was quick as well wasn't slow at all had a little power like he had it modified for his purpose of entertainment. I'd seen Mandy with Jammy Sammy a few times but never really knew who she was until one night I and Scott are walking through the dark rat-infested alleyways of the red light district up to no good when we got spooked by Jammy Sammy jumping out on us from a blind spot, it was a bad idea for Jammy Sammy because Scott used to carry a little black pocket flick butterfly knife for protection just in case we got stuck up again because it had already happened previously so we had to feel protected, I had a little black cosh and it was good that we carried those because life was real and bad things could happen to you at any time especially being small young semi vulnerable bigger guys in the city that are doing the same shit as us would try to test you so you had to be ready and keep your eyes open at all times.

As Jammy Sammy jumps out of this dark spot Scott pulls his knife and goes to stab Jammy Sammy straight away but realises it's Jammy Sammy who instantly shouts "it is me, it's me" with the shadow of Mandy behind him in tow, Scott shouts at Jammy Sammy for his prank and says don't do that shit you could've just got stabbed you fool while I'm in the background laughing as I think it was a nervous one from the fright I just received from Jammy Sammy jumping out on me but Scott wasn't so happy at all. I knew Mandy was something different from the average woman because of how she dressed and from watching tv programs like (BAND OF GLOD) I could tell she was into prostitution, short skirt, lipstick, makeup, high heels, long fake painted fingernails with her dirty looking blonde unkempt hair she fit the part for a roll in (BAND OF GOLD).

Randy Mandy as I named her was ruthless, She and Jammy Sammy were like a team Bonnie & Clyde type always into some shit always committing the crime and getting into confrontations with people in public robbing & stealing the punters for their money and material possessions.

The scheme was to use Mandy as bait to lure punters to a secret location of any kind out of sight from the watching eyes of the public so using the back streets of the city was the best place to be especially to carry out robberies & any other attacks It was the right idea because most punters didn't do anything blatant they'd rather do their business in private where nobody can see which was better for us because that's where they feel more comfortable with what they are doing but at the same time Scott and I would keep an eye Jammy Sammy to prevent him from causing serious harm to people because he was a raving lunatic.

Mandy would walk up and down the strip and stand on the corners showing off most of her skin enticing all the horny men to choose her instead of the many other working women while we'd wait behind the scenes keeping an eye on her in a distance, even though Mandy was the way she was we found ourselves looking after her at the same time because she became something like a blessing in many ways very useful plus it was Jammy Sammy who schooled us also shown us certain things plus it's Jammy Sammy who introduced us to her and told us she'll make us a lot of money if we treat her right but being young the naivety of our minds didn't understand and didn't soak up the game we were given also didn't realise until we learned and studied the game for ourselves that sex is a powerful drug a money maker.

As I watched Mandy & Jammy Sammy orchestrate their plan I was amazed at how much money they would make in just a couple of hours or so by robbing punters, they must have made around £500-£1000 a night doing this shit and don't forget it was Mandy's occupation to be up and down that strip daily morning noon & night so most of these punters could have caught her at any time because they knew where they could find her but I think she felt safe that Jammy Sammy and we had her back which we did without question.

Thinking back now to when I was in that era of time I didn't realise Jammy Sammy was pimping Mandy, by making her have sex and act out sexual content to the punters but then again that was her life so I guess she enjoyed doing that also she had to do it so she could pay for her addiction so in my eyes she never saw anything wrong with the way Jammy Sammy treated her which is a shame because deep down she was a good woman she was just a lost soul and found herself an inner deeper hole to where she was trapped which felt like the abyss and the point of no return.

Understanding about the underground sex industry at the age of nine years old seems very hard to believe probably for many people, without me running away from home and wanting to be on the streets I never would have seen those things that I was seeing at nine years old.

I put myself in that position because it was me who wanted to, I guess a little bit off influences from films and other people but all in all, it was me and only me and

I kind of liked the nightlife it became something like a drug to me I loved the streets I think I may have loved them a little bit too much. Mandy blessed me with some game and told me running away from home ain't good an that I should go back home to my mum the streets don't love you it ain't safe out here, I told her my worries as a child and told her the main reason I went of the rails and started getting into trouble with the police and not wanting to go school.

I explained it started due to my mums' boyfriend Trevor Dailey passing who was like a father to me and it affected me emotionally and it was that emotion that I couldn't handle and the fact that I'd never see him again, I guess I couldn't speak to my mum at the time about my feelings because I was just running away from it and that's why doing what I was doing made it better in some way but not realising that I'm making my life worse.

She sat me down and told me one day about her life because I used to ask her all the time why her life has turned out like it has and the reasons behind being into drugs and prostitution I understood what she was saying to a certain extent but I was still confused and needed more than just knowing her as "Mandy".

She explained and went into detail about herself for me to get an understanding of her as the person she went on to say that her parents passed away when she was a little girl so she grew up with her grandmother to then

lose her grandmother to cancer than to grow up in foster care which sent her head a little mad than had a few
problems being admitted in and out of a foster house's
being admitted in & out of the hospital due to ill health
to overcome that then meet a guy in her early twenties
who was abusing his power with her then to fall pregnant to then have a stillborn which then sent her into a
depressive state of mind plus the loss of her child effected
her that much she's been a working girl & on drugs ever
since. It's a sad story which many of the women working
the street can relate to, in some cases it's easier said than
done for some because the mental state of mind can play
tricks on you and if ain't headstrong and got the ability
to overcome certain obstacles you'll forever fall victim to
the devil's influences. At the age of nine running away
from home and committing the crime had a negative
effect but also had a positive effect through the eyes of
mine because many things in this life can't be taught at
school so the reality of life is on the street not through
the tv screen you can watch as many films as many tv
programs as you want but the reality is until you see it for
yourself you'll forever be blind to the real world and how
certain things are a how situations can evolve and your
whole life can change in a blink of an eye. Tv only shows
you fictional characters that play out what occurs in real
life, so when I saw it first hand for myself visually it was
much different from watching (BAND OF GOLD) or any

other film or program this shit was real life I witnessed with my own eyes people suffering sleeping rough on the floor between shop doorways with cardboard boxes as mattresses punters getting stabbed by the pimps because they've taken the piss out of one of their girls and not paid them the right money a lot of shit was going on it was dangerous.

I saw pretty much all kinds of madness at an early age on the streets of the red light district also within the streets of Manchester itself, Manchester is a beautiful place generally nice people a good tourist attraction for people all over the world history dates back centuries from the Manchester theatre's & cathedrals and lost roads buried from canals that sweep through the city and home to the first international trade exports license destination in the world, despite the history and the lovable nature of the people Manchester also has a dark side that can be nightmarishly frightening so if you ain't careful and not switched on you could meet your demise.

The robbing continued for some time in and out of restaurants and office buildings taking anything we could and taking it back to Jammy Sammy who would sell it on for us for a profitable piece of the pie for himself, I didn't mind whatsoever because one thing I can say Jammy Sammy never once ripped us off maybe a few times where I thought I didn't get what I wanted but that was probably due to a quick sale or we lost it, maybe on the backhand he did do the dirty on me and Scott and pocketed a few of the extras for himself but I can say he ever robbed us blatantly he kept it real despite being a drug addict.

Overall Jammy Sammy was a good guy he looked like one of those working types crack addicts who took it recreationally as he didn't look scruffy he looked after himself dressed decently and presented himself in a good way so maybe that's why he didn't look suspicious or thought off as a threat to anyone which gave him the upper hand when it came to doing business which makes sense for the reason his nickname being (Jammy Sammy).

Unfortunately; for (Jammy Sammy) his past caught up with him and found him overdosing on a bad batch of heroin. Mandy was with him at the time when it happened and when she told us the following day she said he was just Chilling next minute he went into some sort of epileptic fit she tried her best to try and save him but there was nothing she could have done plus she was wanted by the police so she couldn't phone the authorities she was in a sticky situation.

She explained that he was complaining about pains in his chest a few days before but didn't go to the doctors to get checked just took it as a smokers cough and little cold and didn't do anything about it, as bad as is it was, In the end, she said she had to leave (Jammy Sammy) in some crack den in Ancoats close to the town centre she called the emergency services anonymously from the payphone told them where they could find Jammy Sammy and that he's overdosed on drugs.

It was a big loss losing Jammy Sammy literally, he was the backbone of the wheels that drove our whole operation well Mandy to but he was responsible for the way certain things moved & worked because we didn't have the links and knowledge that he did plus he was the auctioneer as well as Mandy's support too it was a difficult thing that she had to do already coping and dealing with her problems in life, it's heartbreaking as well as heartwarming because we're all human beings at the end of the day and we all have our demons to fight so we shouldn't pass judgment on others before knowing them because you never know what another person's life experiences have been like for them to have made that difficult decisions I'm sure many can relate to Mandy.

Mandy, Scott & I continued robbing the punters which became a more regular thing for income because the restaurants were getting on to the fact that their stock was getting robbed so they started locking up stuff so you weren't able to steal the food and cases of liquor anymore it was much more difficult.

Luring the punters to our designated low key spots was essential due to the nightlife being occupied by civilians going about their daily lives.

But under the darkness of the darkened cloudy blue skies of Manchester along with the pissy rat-infested graffitied alleyways of the red light district was the best place to stick the punters up and strip them for their dignity & possessions as well as anything else which was appetising to us.

The underground industry of a working girls sex life can be life-threatening.

Seeing for myself as well as being involved in multiple accounts of dangerous situations is rarely seen as a 9-year-old child, to some people it must be shocking to hear and hard to comprehend that I was seeing this shit and certain people might think what about my parents but my mum ain't to blame I've made my own choices & decisions it was me who was choosing to behave in that way.

Thinking back to those crazy moments of my young life taking serious risks takes a little time for me to digest it and believe that I'm still alive to tell my story I do believe in some way I'm here for a reason. because sometimes when you went to rob a punter that's paying a working girl for sex or any sort of sexual act you would get the odd few that would have their protection and be brave enough to defend themselves; whether that was pulling out a bladed article or some sort of metal pole you just couldn't predict what anyone would do most importantly you couldn't underestimate anyone the last thing that you want to do is judge someone by the way they looked because I've been there and seen it with my own eyes when certain punters look fragile but have acted out of fear.

Because when people get scared "adrenaline" kicks in and I've been in many dangerous situations where knives have been drawn so you had to be very careful in that field of work it wasn't something to be taken lightly or taken advantage off you could fall victim very fast especially if you weren't street smart.

Plus what you have to remember is "everybody" is wired different nobody is the same plus not all people are gonna react in the same way some maybe be in a state of shock "freeze" up and stay in fright, whereas others are going to want to fight and take a flight a do whatever it takes to get them out off that situation because it's life or death in those streets it's a vicious cycle of violence in the underground sex industry.

After Jammy Sammy passed I could see that Mandy was very different wasn't around that much instead of seeing her on the strip mostly every night it became a few nights a week that we would see her. The game we took from Jammy Sammy and the knowledge he gave us helped us along the way and carried us through without him I'd say we would off been stuck so I only can appreciate and respect him for that despite anything he was a good guy just another lost soul in the world that made a few bad decisions in life rest in eternal peace Jammy Sammy.

Crime started getting a bit difficult to do in the red light district plus the punters were a lot warier about picking the girls in case they got attacked and robbed plus the police were out in force cracking down started taking all the little spots away by putting warning signs up plus the council started boarding up all the derelict buildings that were used as crack dens and hiding spots. Me, Scott Street & my other friend Antwon Elson slowly drifted apart by this time because I was on the verge of going into care due to my behaviour and had been arrested on multiple occasions whilst being under the watchful eye of the authorities so things weren't looking too bright for me at this point.

I never saw Mandy ever again for no reason other than I wasn't around much like how I was normally I was going through the process of courts because of my none attendance to education and all the criminal activities plus gang associates, as a young man I couldn't handle emotional stress so all the negative feelings I had plus all the shit I had to go through with the authorities is what I was running away from.

Plus getting picked up on the streets of Manchester late at night at times by the authorities don't sit well with social services because anything I'd done or had been doing was getting reported and logged written down and stored in the cabinet for future reference.

As you have read my care history the emotional stress had an impact and moulded my life especially being influenced by many things, not just the people, my story is to raise awareness and give people my views & opinions and the way I see it and to give people a piece of my experience and for you to put yourself in my shoes walk with me see it through my eyes.

Everybody has their individuality the quality of being different the uniqueness of a person makes our personalities differ from the other human beings and we're able to think for ourselves, so whatever we decide to do were just going to do it, making mistakes is an essential part of life without making those mistakes you will never know how to solve or overcome the challenges you're faced with and one of the most selfish traits that humans carry is judging the things that others have done without putting themselves in their shoes to understand the reality of other peoples situations where they've made choices that ain't worked out the way they wished it would. Nobody has the right to pass judgement on anyone but then again it's a cruel world plus we live in a world full of opinionated people those that make comments are usually from the people who ain't lived a troubled life tend to feel more negative and it's those that are considered the contradictories to the minority of society, I believe, nobody is born "perfect".

Canal Street has existed since the early 1800s, became a red-light district in the 1960s, and still stands today but its atmosphere attracts a different kind of clientele now with gay clubs & bars very different set up from the late 1990s.

In Great Britain (England, Wales and Scotland), the act of engaging in sex as part of an exchange of sexual services for money is legal, but several related activities, including soliciting in a public place, kerb-crawling, owning or managing a brothel, pimping and pandering, are crimes.

SELF DESTRUCTIVE BEHAVIOUR.

I'm not long coming out of the care system still not attending education and my behaviour is still wild not learned anything from the last few years of being in care, I'm now rebellious on the streets.

The crime rate was on the rise naturally throughout the city and at this point, I'm 13 14 years old still not going to education committing crime after crime getting arrested for multiple thefts and carjackings.

Although on most occasions, being ruthless is considered, a bad thing, there are plenty of situations imaginable where ruthlessness can be a good thing. It can be a good strategy, as long as it is part of a broader mindset of how you choose to interact with other people.

One thing that affected me was knowing that my mum was the victim of an assault when she was out one night with my auntie they were walking to the venue when some black guy popped out of the shadows and snatched her handbag, I'm not sure if she fell or maybe just got slightly injured but I know she was a bit shook up because of that incident.

That made me worse as a child growing up knowing some scumbag tried robbed my mum for her handbag and what little she had plus those two incidents where I fell victim myself to street robbery ×2 I wasn't happy whatsoever and I carried hate and anger towards everybody especially males, any man would get robbed or any boy I'd see on a good bike that would get robbed anything left outside the shops would get taken I was taking anything and everything I liked no ifs no buts if I wanted it I'd take it was just as simple as that.

Self-destructive actions include intentional self-harm by cutting or engaging in reckless behaviour, such as going on a hunger strike.

Self-destruction and attempting suicide are usually extreme measures used in an attempt of alleviating emotional distress.

I was suicidal at an early age but I personally never resulted in cutting myself or harm myself in that way especially to make myself bleed my self-destruction behaviour was more crime and criminal related, not self-harming.

Lying, cheating, stealing, and violent behaviour are some common destructive behaviours. There are many reasons why these behaviours occur, including getting out of a tough situation, raising self-esteem, gaining possessions, frustration, anger, provocation, and chemical influence.

They say you're more prone to behave in a self-destructive manner if you've experienced: alcohol or drug use. childhood trauma, neglect, or abandonment, emotional or physical abuse. I did experience most of these traumatic things in my young life which explains why my focus was more towards the streets and doing crimes, plus weed was my go too when I was feeling stressed as well as getting love from the hustles gangsters and thugs on the block.

There was nothing more indulging than being around the older niggaz on the block because they made me feel comfortable blessed no matter what I did I was blessed they treated me with respect and like I was their younger brother.

But I was on self-destruction going through all of the above plus courts the effects of losing loved ones my life was out of control only if I would have taken the time to listen to what was being said to me I would have directed my energy on bettering myself but situations arose and the streets just kept on pulling me in I was addicted. It was inevitable that later on down the line continuing not to go education robbing cars smoking weed thieving selling drugs and fucking around with firearms and gangs, that I would be rather dead or locked up doing football numbers or maybe even doing life behind bars.

And that's what most certainly happened to me so kids not to be a hypocrite but the message stays in school stay educated stay away from the negativity stay around positive folks people who have your own personal best interest at heart, don't waste your time focusing on the bad things in life there is a beautiful world out there and it's there for you to explore it beautiful birds ain't meant to be caged spread your wings. LIVE 3.

CHAPTER SEVEN

Gangs.
Blood on the Concrete.

The original tragic teenage troublemakers, 'The Scuttlers' used everything from belt buckles to broken bottles to beat their rivals. But when beatings turned to killings, their days were numbered.

"This city continues to assert itself as a centre for brutality and violence almost without rival throughout England".

A contemporary account of Manchester in the second half 19th Century

The Victorian Greater Manchester area was one of the world's first industrial conurbations. From the turn of the 19th century, hundreds of thousands of families had flooded in, attracted by the area's 1,600 textile works.

By 1870, such as the level of output, that the city was often covered in sulphurous smog. But that couldn't hide the extreme poverty that accompanied this explosive industrial growth.

The factory districts that sprung up in the shadows of the red brick mill buildings saw conditions comparable to today's worst third world country slums.

Manchester's Moss Side made national headlines regularly during the 1980s and '90s, giving the city an unsavoury reputation for gangs and gun crime.

However, over a century earlier, young men with striking uniforms of bell-bottom trousers, heavy brass buckled belts, silk scarves and brass-tipped clogs terrorised the city's streets, committing horrifying acts of violence.

This was how Britain's first youth cult – before Birmingham's Peaky Blinders – the Scuttlers emerged from the grimy streets of 1870s industrial Manchester.

Gangs such as the Bengal Tigers (from Bengal Street in Ancoats), the Meadow Lads (from Angel Meadow) and the Grey Mare Boys (from Grey Mare Lane) were armed with knives and belt buckles, ready to wage ferocious turf wars with their enemies.

SLUM CITIES.

The area's back streets were a warren of horrendously overcrowded back to back lodgings, teeming tenements, workhouses, beer-houses, brothels and dosshouses. Tuberculosis ran rampant. Parental control was difficult in homes so small that even sleeping space was limited. With no room inside, life had to be lived on the street.

Which, to be fair, making it a vibrant place. These were streets full of music halls and gin shops. But whatever the resilient character of its people, these were still slums. One of the worst in the area, indeed in the world at that time, was the Ancoats; 'one of the foulest creations of the new Industrial Age'. This 'chimney of the world' was surveyed in 1889 and half of its families were defined as 'very poor. And Karl Marx's co-author of 'The Communist Manifesto', Friedrich Engels, named Salford a classic world slum.

Other areas such as Angel Meadow and Collyhurst were equally squalid and grim. With so little space, territorial fights soon became common all over Manchester.

ERA OF THE HARD KNOCKS.

Some argue they were simply mirroring the British Empire. In part fuelled by the Manchester factories, the British were nearly always at war.

They were constantly trying to enlarge their territories, fighting everywhere from Africa to Afghanistan.

But according to historian Andrew Davies, it was the sectarian underbelly of the 1870 Franco Prussian war (Catholic France versus Protestant Germany) that captured the imagination of many on the streets of Manchester. It mirrored the divisions between the recent Irish immigrants and their established and unwelcoming English neighbours.

Heroic stories of this conflict were told in schools and when the boys left education aged just 12, some of the more testosterone-fuelled tried to mimic them. Gang warfare broke out on the slum streets. For these boys with few employment prospects, recreational violence was always an option.

The gangs provided status, excitement and respect to individuals who had little.

Soon, one sound would cut through the din of factory machinery and strike fear into the residents of even those hardened cobbled streets: The clatter of the brass tipped clogs of the scuttlers.

THE FIRST YOUTH CULTS/

MANCHESTER GANGS.

The scuttlers, the slang name given to these street fighting gangs, originally emerged from Ancoats and Angel Meadow.

They then spread across the river to Salford's Adelphi and Greengate districts.

What differentiates them from gangs of youths throughout history was their particular attention to style.

They used soap as a hair gel to flatten down their long fringes over the left eye, the so-called 'donkey fringe'. The hair on their back and sides was closely cropped. They often sported neckerchiefs or flashy patterned scarves. The flaps of their coat pockets were cut into peaks and were buttoned down. They wore bell-bottomed trousers, like a sailor's, and some had pointed, metal-tipped clogs on their feet. This wasn't a simple fashion statement as they would inflict a more grievous wound when kicking a rival. Each gang had its distinctive colours and look. This attention to appearance served a practical purpose. In the heat of battle, it helped distinguish friend from foe.

Such dress also signalled to outsiders that this was no ordinary working-class lad. This was a street fighter. This was a scuttler. It was this conscious differentiation of themselves that's partly behind why Andrew Davies, the definitive historian of these Manchester gangs, subtitles his book, 'Britain's First Youth Cult'. The good people of Manchester would not be the first, or the last, to be panicked and outraged at the spectacle of lawless, sadistic, uncontrollable packs of teenagers. Many were not the amoral, almost orphaned denizens of the street as portrayed by the press. Most were in employment, in contrast to their counterparts, the Cornermen of Liverpool. At home, they would be expected to and did contribute to the family income. So when scuttlers ended up in court, it was often their mothers who came to plead as to their previous good character. And that the family could not afford the loss of a wage earner if their son were jailed.

When a Manchester Guardian journalist interviewed four members of an Ancoats gang in 1898, he found them articulate, amusing and refreshingly respectful. Some got in trouble with the law for nothing more than gambling or bathing in the wrong canal.

Their ages ranged from 12 to 20, and though their violent acts were criminal, these weren't professional criminals motivated by making money illegally.

They were working-class thrill-seeking teenagers.

The Scuttlers were members of neighbourhood-based youth gangs (known as scuttling gangs) formed in working-class areas of Manchester, Salford, and the surrounding townships during the late 19th century. It is possible to draw parallels with the London street gangs of the 1890s, whose behaviour was labelled hooligans. The social commentator Alexander Devine attributed the gang culture to lack of parental control, lack of discipline in schools, "base literature" and the monotony of life in Manchester's slums. Gangs were formed throughout the slums of central Manchester, in the townships of Bradford, Gorton, and Openshaw to the east and Salford, to the west of the city. Gang conflicts erupted in Manchester in the early 1870s and went on sporadically for 30 years, declining in frequency and severity by the late 1890s.

Scuttlers distinguished themselves from other young men in working-class neighbourhoods by their distinctive clothing. They generally wore a uniform of brass-tipped pointed clogs, and bell-bottomed trousers cut like a sailor's ("bells" that measured fourteen inches around the knee and twenty-one inches round the foot) and "flashy" silk scarves. Their hair was cut short at the back and sides, but they grew long fringes, known as "donkey fringes", that were longer on the left side and plastered down on the forehead over the left eye. Peaked caps were also worn tilted to the left to display the fringe. The scuttlers' girlfriends also had a distinctive style of dress consisting of clogs, shawl, and a vertically striped skirt. Scuttling gangs were territorial fighting gangs, as reflected in their names; the Bengal Tigers came from the cluster of streets and courts off Bengal Street in Ancoats. Most gangs took their names from a local thoroughfare, such as Holland Street, Miles platting or Hope Street, Salford. Gang members fought with a variety of weapons, but they all carried knives and wore heavy buckled belts, often decorated with pictures such as serpents, scorpions, hearts pierced with arrows or women's names. The thick leather belts were their most prized possessions and were wrapped tightly around the wrist at the onset of a "scuttle" so that the buckle could be used to strike at opponents. The use of knives and belts was designed to maim and disfigure rather than to kill.

Some of the clashes between rival gangs involved large numbers; described one such instance in May 1879 as involving more than 500 people. Scuttling reached a peak in 1890–91; it was said that by 1890 more youths were held in Strangeways prison for scuttling than for any other offence. By the turn of the century, the gangs had all but died out owing to some of the worst slums having been cleared, the setting up of Working Lads' Clubs (such as Salford lads club) to engage the working youths in more peaceful activities, the spread of street football and the advent of the cinema.

One initiative to provide an alternative to gang warfare resulted in the formation of St Marks (West Gorton) Football Club, which later became Manchester City.

After doing a lot of research retaining the information not solely for myself but to give knowledge to the readers.

In 1997 the Manchester historian Gary James highlighted that scuttling was the number one unifying activity of young men and that the creation of St Mark's Football Club was a very serious attempt at diverting the young men of West Gorton into more worthwhile activities.

Anna Connell, perceived by many as the founder of St Mark's FC, also helped create men's meetings, a library, and other society improving facilities and clubs.

Manchester gangs date back to the late 1880, of the Victorian times with the Scuttlers as you just read a little history.

But as the years went by with the Caribbean culture struggling to find work especially within the early 1980s when everybody in England felt the impact of the recession crisis when employment fell dramatically and the whole English economy went into a state of panic.

It appears gun crime in Manchester begun in the 1970s at a time of rising unemployment and poverty in the area, which is known as a centre of Manchester's black British Afro Caribbean community finding it difficult to make a living from legitimate means some residents chose to turn to the drug trade – mainly the sale of cannabis instead of hard drugs.

Most of the drug conflict was centred around the Moss Side precinct where black British youths would sell cannabis or heroin & crack cocaine.

During the early 1990s, the use of firearms by criminals in south Manchester soared along with gang associations.

Gangs related to their 'patch', named after places such as Gooch Close, & Doddington Close.

South Manchester's gangs became engaged in feuds with each other for the control of the drug trade and also respect for the community they lived in.

Shootings and murders increased in frequency in the years in different areas, not all were recorded as gang-related. This started attracting negative news and media headlines, with Manchester being given the nickname 'Gunchester' used, to sum up, this increase in gang, drugs & firearms activity.

Gun-related violence featured throughout the 1990s. In January 1993, 14-year-old Benji Stanley was shot dead as he queued for an Alvino's takeaway on Greatwestern street Moss Side. The reasons surrounding his death are not fully known and no one has ever been prosecuted for his tragic murder which is going to be heartbreaking for the family because losing a child at 14 years old the emotional distress must be unbearable but then again on the flip side it's how things go in the hood sometimes but no mother should be burying their child no matter their age it's sad and nine times out of ten it is because of mistaken identity being recognised for somebody else.

During the mid-1990s, the police started developing new approaches to confronting gun crime in south Manchester which was initially met with limited success.

These started with Operation China in the mid-1990s, which aimed at targeting gang members and taking them out of circulation a lot got caught and birded off but it was still rife but not as bad.

By the late 1990s gun-related killings had increased with the nature of shootings changing becoming more reckless often seeming to take place over petty disputes, such as a row over a "girl" or ownership of a bike/car etc, surprisingly, rarely over the drug dealing "turf".

The stats have shown in 1996 saw 28 confirmed shootings with 12 wounded and four dead. In 1997 there were 68 confirmed shootings, with 39 injuries and six deaths. In 1999 more shots were fired in the Manchester area than in any other year, after doing my research at least

270 reported shootings (based on found shell casings), with the majority being in the south Manchester areas of Longsight, Moss Side and Hulme.

In 1999 there were 43 gun-related injuries and seven fatalities.

Even though I was only a young man seeing the effects of the gang life that surrounded me and seeing the damage it caused not only on myself but on the families of the deceased, as well as the community, wasn't a good experience.

It was truly scary being a young 9 10-year-old man, and hearing those gunshots on your estate wasn't pleasant either and being in a position where you can find yourself staring in the eyes of death just by being in the wrong place at the wrong time. Being around the influences of alcohol drugs & gangs at that age was another reason for the authorities to keep me from my home town of Manchester and eventually placing me in the hands of strangers and care plus when I was coming home for the weekend, I remember I was 11 year's old and I went to visit my good friend (C-loc) and we were kicking in the hairdressers called classic cuts, Rusholme chatting with one of the older g's whilst the barber was cutting his hair.

He got a fresh cut spoke to us for a few minutes gave us ten pounds each and rode off in the direction of Moss Side we were happy to see him as well as over the moon that he blessed us ten pounds each 2 fresh crispy notes that would have given you a paper cut, a few moments later like no longer than 5 minutes gunshots echoed in the distance as we ran to the road to see what was going on I couldn't see anything and I didn't even have the thought of anything bad happening to my people. Not even 10-15 minutes, had passed, when blue lights racing down Great Western street towards the direction of Moss Side. As we got around the corner from where (C-loc) lived we saw one of our family members crying absolutely in a rage of pain and suffering and I could see it in her eyes it wasn't a good thing for me to witness, as we got closer we realised that it was the older G that had been shot the atmosphere felt cold everybody was rushing and running around talking fast and as an 11-year-old boy it broke my heart in a million pieces he was a good man, had a heart of gold.

It was Remi Martins, tragic death that made me carry a lot of hate to the opposition and it was at this stage in my young life in 1999 when I was wanting to purchase a firearm to get revenge against the people who were responsible for the loss of a good man a family man a well-respected individual in the community. Honestly, in my opinion, a lot of people shouldn't have to die and a lot of people don't deserve to perish but when a loved one gets taken away from you especially for no real reason other than people ain't got the heart to fight or have a conversation to settle their differences between themselves as a result of that, people die and when you're a kid growing up in that environment and having to be a part of that things just happen out of emotional distress.

Early In 2001 if I can recall a multi-agency approach to tackling gun crime was initiated when the Manchester Multi-Agency Gang Strategy (MMAGS) was introduced as a result of the Home office 1999 Tilley and Bullock report.

A new approach to tackling gun crime began to develop with police working more closely with the local community and other agencies within the surrounding area.

The high rate of shooting incidents continued into the early 2000s, though gradually the number of gun murders declined to a much lower rate.

April 2004 saw panic at Manchester Royal infirmary as rival gang members spotted each other after a shooting and found themselves brawling which police had to be called and a few of us got arrested that day but it's part of the game when gooch and Doddington collide anybody that was there or heard about it would tell you it's funk on sight.

There have been many sad deaths with young men falling victim to gun crime with the likes of young Benji Stanley 13 years old, 16 years old, Luis Brathwaite, 15-year-old Jessie James who was tragically killed on the 9th September 2006, from what I read he was cycling home from a party with friends and was shot and I believe died in hospital from his injuries.

He was the youngest victim since Benji Stanley, his was also believed to be a case of mistaken identity, with the community maintaining he wasn't involved in any of the area's gang and drug-related activities it's a shame that another teenager meets his demise, being a pattern of Similarities with the lack of witnesses willing to come forward has prevented his killers being identified and brought to justice which is more sad news for the family & relatives of the deceased.

In January 2007 when I was doing my 10-year bid in prison for a gang-related shooting I read an article in the manchester evening news and they reported a 'consistent decrease' in firearms incidents over two years, which is attributed to the work of the Xcalibre gang unit, Greater Manchester Police's specialist task force.

I believe Xcalibre received a funding boost of £6.5 million in June 2008.

Reading the article the police spokesman said something like the recent "Operation Cougar has had a "massive impact" on gang-related shootings in the area and it was hoped the new money would help build on that success".

I was sat in prison thinking it's a waste of taxpayers money despite anything because they'll always be gang-related crime no matter what, many people have lost their relationships with some of the closest people in their lives so there living in a dream world if they think gang warfare will cease it will never cease it will be a continuous cycle of emotional pain and distress.

I was thinking they have no idea it's deeper than just pumping money into tackling gang-related crime there's a bigger picture, there's poverty, broken homes, kids losing their innocence to child neglect. Some kids are growing up with no dads plus kids living in poverty coming from broken homes as well as losing uncles & brothers to the gun crime for so many reasons and not all circumstances are gang-related there's the conflict of interest, disrespect, paranoia, jealousy, impaired decision making because of drugs or alcohol abuse there are many symptoms regarding the effects of gang life (P.T.S.D) is the biggest killer of men involved in violence like a war veteran trying to block out all the bloodshed and the loss of friends killed in action.

(Young Gooch Crew) known as "Y.G.C" was formed by the offspring of the older generation which gained a powerful reputation for the violence and guns we used. Knifes wasn't our style whereas the thought of getting shot doesn't sound too bad but getting stabbed, well, that's more personal plus I kind of had a phobia about knives when I was young so I'd rather get shot than stabbed and I'm sure many people have the same thought process if they had to choose between the two being in that life.

I remember being a kid when five homies were arrested following Operation Eagle and were sentenced to more than 43 years in prison.

Us as the Young Gooch continued the war with the newly emerging Longsight Crew, (L.S.C) a younger off-shoot of the Doddington gang whose members were based on many estates in the Longsight and Ardwick areas of south Manchester, especially their headquarters of Langport Avenue which we targeted most times.

By the mid-2000s us being the young Gooch had grown to become a vast gang having alliances with several smaller offshoot crews based around south Manchester.

The most notable of these being the Old Trafford Crips which was formed in the early '00s, Rusholme Man Dem R.M.D, & the Fallowfield Mad Dogs also known as (F.M.D).

Even though we were from different sides we were on different levels of banging I had a lot of respect & time for folks up in the Fallowfield section they weren't shy they got it cracking only a selected few though but without going into any names they'll know who they are and they know it's nothing but love from the ground up we'll forever be locked in.

We had a good relationship with many but not all but the ones we were close to would carry on the rivalry with Doddington and the Longsight Crew plus they needed to protect what was there's too, although certain individuals weren't even gang members but were friends of friends from the same area that would inevitably get you into trouble.

After all, you couldn't just get seen or hang with certain people and be cool it would cause problems for certain people even being related to individuals resulted in getting labelled affiliated, so because of their affiliations to us they had to protect themselves because I don't think anyone wants to get bullied or be treated like a punk especially in the hood bad news travels fast.

There were a few of the homeboys that got shot early in the '00s and I was with one of them one day on the estate when the rivals came through the block on pedal bikes and let off a couple of shots hitting my friend in his thigh just above the ass cheek, we fled the scene with the sound of ringing shots blasting from what sounded like a mini air bomb giving my friend who got shot the assistance over the wall.

I made sure he was good then fled from the scene to avoid the police because I knew they would have been wanting answers about the shooting but I didn't have time for them to be asking me shit I was off I wasn't sticking around to found out.

I had genuine love & respect for my people so to protect them felt like the right thing to do especially at that time because I'm not going to let my people be treated in any way without me defending those that are at risk of danger by the hands-off others it's not going to happen it was certainly a no brainer for me no questions asked whatsoever my loyalty came second to none I took my friendship very seriously.

Even though I was classed as a gang member through the eyes of the authorities and other gang members, I didn't see it that way and many other people from my community didn't see me in that light either I was respected in the community in the sense of protecting parents kids from harm.

After all, there's been plenty of times when kids would get robbed for their bikes not just by our rivals but by different people from different areas and id found out who it was and get them back plus I had respect for the people within my community because they showed me nothing but love since I was growing up as a kid plus I love my home town there is nothing I wouldn't do for my place of birth, Manchester is where my heart is.

There were many shootouts that I had myself maybe a couple with a few close homies but overall it was just me on my own experience doing crazy shit making sure that people knew not to fuck with me or my team I think that was more on the grounds of not having any older brothers to run too I saw my strap as was my bigger brother you disrespected me or any older man felt like putting their hands on me well, let's just say it wouldn't have been a great day for them I most certainly would off blown their head of their shoulders and not worried or cared too much about them.

Gun thugs get 19 years for street shooting that's what the headline says:

TWO teenage gunmen have been caged for 19 years for their roles in a turf war shooting that left a rival gang member with a gunshot wound to his head which resulted from him being blind in one eye.

Aaron Grossman, 17 at the time and 18-year-old Lance Houghton-Savage were both members of the Young Gooch Close mob - whose rivalry with the Doddington Gang has plagued the streets of Manchester for many years.

On that Sunday of the 31st Halloween 2004 we organised to meet up the following morning where we spoke about our plan and how we going to orchestrate the plan etc, I armed myself with my weapon of choice which was the .38 revolver Smith & Wesson snub nose and my homie had the sawn-off shotgun that held 7 bores known as double R's we took a trip over to the rivals side and I remember it being a bright day a sunny winter's morning around 9:30 am a little bit cold but a fresh morning as you can imagine winter mornings at that time the streets are quiet but we're up the early crack of dawn getting active as they say "the early bird catches the worm".

We decided to walk instead of driving or biking it because that's what we would normally be the option but this time we felt walking like I said it was a fresh day so we decided to hotfoot it instead.

We stopped at our friends' crib which was a bit iffy because he lived right on Doddington territory but that's where his mum lived and I always thought it was a bit weird because for someone to be associated with the opposite side but live on their estate without feeling a bit uneasy didn't sit well with me I couldn't do that, but each to their own and I don't think there's anything you can do if it's where your mum lives.

We landed at our destination where his mum and family was his mum cooking Sunday dinner with her reggae tunes on in the background it was the typical black household vibe on early Sunday morning. We spoke a word and explained to him we were heading over to the rival side on a mission are you looking to roll he replied "No" a few more words was exchanged between us but didn't stop any longer than 10 15 minutes and we was out the door with murder on our mind.

We hot-footed with guns concealed walking for about 15 minutes when I spotted a Renault Megan sport which I have seen on our estate speeding and hitting corners crazy a few nights before, I could tell it was their car because the seats were way back.

Getting closer to the car as I looked through the drivers' side window and noticed there were keys left in the ignition so I opened the door jumped in and tried to start the car but as I went to put it in gear it would jerk cut out and stall.

I was pissed off that it didn't start so I jumped on the bonnet and put my foot through the window-screen I was more upset that I couldn't ride on them punks in their car but it wouldn't start so I chose the 2nd option and smashed all the windows and kept it pushing forward.

I heard shouting coming from out the car that stopped at top of the road and I could see it was being driven by a prominent member of the Doddington gang as we approached closer with our guns out he sped off as I aimed my .38 at the car ready to let one go hoping to hit him or whoever that he was in the car with.

We ran to the top of the road to see where it had gone plus to get over the other side of the road and to get off the side street just in case they tried to ambush us from the blindside, we hit a couple of alleyways to avoid being seen not just by our rivals but civilians because we had our guns out in plain sight ready for action we and found ourselves back in the territory of the Doddington Estate which was ideal coz I wasn't leaving until I shot somebody.

I could hear car tyres screeching round bends in the distance also the sound of car doors slamming like people are hopping out to try to catch us by surprise suddenly out of nowhere I saw this black figure running towards me with a black handgun in his hand immediately with no hesitation he started squeezing.

"BANG" "BANG" "BANG" "BANG" "BANG" about 4 to 5 shots heading in my direction I could sparks of the wall as one of the bullets bounced off the concrete not panicking as much because I had safety with my armour-plated bulletproof vest which I had strapped to my chest I hid behind the wall waiting for him to make an appearance with my .38 revolver out ready to blast him. As the bangs ended which lasted no longer than a few seconds I realised he didn't pop up so I looked around the wall and noticed that he was gone as he has just done a magic trick we ran to the top of the street when a car was careening towards us on Raby Street, Moss Side.

As residents on their way home from church and the innocence of kids playing innocently watched in horror, a shot was fired from the .38 revolver "BANG" which shattered the window and went straight into the driver's head/eye. I knew I shot him as he sped off in a bid to escape panicking swerving driving erratically, I saw he lost control and crashed into a car that sent him into a building off princess road we were in hot pursuit of firearms out behind them looking to finish the mission.

As I got to the corner of the road I could see them jumping out of the car in the distance running off with one of them holding the other as support stumbling like he's going to collapse as we got closer I saw they were trying to open peoples car doors to hijack their car in a desperate bid to escape. My homie let off the sawn-off 12 gage that was loaded with double R's which rang my ears and left a beeping sound running through my eardrums onlookers watching running taking cover scared looks on their faces they must have thought it was the set of a movie scene but this was real life all I could see was civilian people locking their car doors certain cars speeding through gaps nearly crashing into oncoming traffic speeding through red lights to avoid getting shot it was hectic normal people going about their daily life they must have been terrified thinking back and putting myself in that situation I probably would have done the same at all cost.

We fled the scene as in the distance sirens was ringing out and most definitely it was the armed response unit coming from Greenheys police station not even a mile down the road from the crime that just took place.

As we fled on foot back to the destination of our surroundings we felt more comfortable and relaxed that we were out of the area where the shooting just happened because we knew at that moment there would off been a lot of police activity and most certainly would off been patrolling the local area's.

That very same night we knew it would off been on Granada reports the regional news for our community so because most of us knew what had happened that day we were all waiting for the news to come on to get confirmation if he was dead or alive plus just to hear what the police have to say about the incident itself we were all ears waiting in anticipation.

It's quite sick-minded when I think back to that moment because I remember buying a bottle of liquor (Hennessy) to celebrate that I'd shot a rival and probably killed him as well, I was over the moon it was a feeling I couldn't describe I felt good especially being the person who got shot made it much more worthy for the cause.

What probably contributed to that thought process was the fact I had no regard for human life whatsoever, not even my own I was in the fast lane living that wildlife so to me it was nothing and I felt nothing no emotion whatsoever.

Few weeks had passed since the shooting on that Halloween night of October the 31st 2004. Police were in force on the streets in their Jeep's and vans plus more shootings were still going on at that present time so the streets weren't a good place day or night spontaneous shit would happen it was crazy. I taped off at least 2-3 spots in one day it was too much for the police to handle plus there were no cameras back then so the streets were more dangerous and you were more likely to catch a stray bullet at any time it didn't matter where you were it would be on sight with no if's or buts.

THE BRICK OF EVIDENCE.

That same day of the shooting when the daytime fell to night, and the cloudy skies hovered over the blood-stained streets of south Manchester.

The rivals thought it would be a clever idea to strap a death note tied to a broken half of house brick and throw it against one of my peoples front doors at their address at around 1 a.m. understandably she was scared as any mother would be so she waited for her son to come home that night panicking scared and handed the death note to him and on the note, it said (LIL-A) (BEADLE) & (RIDZ) use are all (DEAD) in red-inked pen.

At this point, he was my homie because don't forget we first went to his house in the morning on the day of the shooting plus I thought he was a solid guy because he was with us hanging and involved in certain activities and was part of the family so to me I didn't think anything of it especially when it came to worrying about him or his mum saying anything to the police. Unknown to me at this time the following morning she took the death note to Green Heys police station and told them that it was thrown against her door the night before and she's worried because her sons' name is on it and she thinks it's something to do with the shooting that took place outside her house few hours before the brick was thrown and she wants to confirm that she's a witness for her son and claims his innocence.

They took the death note for evidence and started to piece together information from house to house inquiries but didn't come up with anything significant to bring any charges to anyone for the shooting which left a man blind in one eye.

Two weeks after the shooting took place in Moss Side the lack of evidence the police had was frustratingly difficult for them because nobody would speak and there were only a few active people that morning going about their daily lives plus there were no shell casings at the scene to give any leads they came to a dead end.

With the death note being there only lead to act on an plus the 2 names being highly active gang members in the streets and being prominent members of the (Y.G.C) also known as (GOOCH) they targeted and put pressure on my homies mum to confirm it was me and (BEADLE) who the death note was referring too, which she clarified to the police which then gave them all the information they needed to make an arrest or at least put us under surveillance.

They watched me and my homie for around a week and I knew they were on to me because I kept seeing dodgy cars outside my mums' house or down the street it seemed everywhere I was going it felt there were eyes on me I knew something wasn't right my gut feeling was trying to tell me something and this was going on for about 7–10 days it wasn't an issue of paranoia.

Because of the lead, they had due to the death note the surveillance gave them more ammunition for evidence because they knew we were involved in gang activities plus a few weeks before the shooting there was a range of shootings in the surrounding area's plus a few of my homeboys had been shot and don't forget at that time Y.G.C had been labelled the most active violent gang and capable of causing serious damage.

I set up cameras around the perimeter of my house front & back, after all, my paranoid thoughts started to kick in and most definitely I had the right to because throughout the week I was seeing all sorts of dodgy shit and was suspicious that the police was watching me.

I still had my .38 Smith & Wesson & .22 derringer plus I had my .357 stashed in an empty house around the corner of where I lived but I had 6 rounds of .357 slugs in a bag together with my .22 & .38 revolver and on the night of the 11th of November 2004, I recall telling my mum to wake me if I fall asleep because I have to do something important.

I remember my mum waking me up that night around 10 o'clock but all I remember after that was waking early hours of the next morning at like 5:30 6 am looking at my camera's to see armed response police right outside my house I jumped out of bed like a "Jack in the box" looked out my bedroom window to see armed police with machine guns and torches pointing in my direction I thought I was dreaming as I wiped the sleep from my eyes my heart sunk as I realised I wasn't dreaming the thought of my firearms in the back garden in my mums rubbish container made it heart race faster.

SUDDENLY "BANG" "BANG" "BANG" ITS THE POLICE OPEN UP, ARMED RESPONSE PUT YOUR HANDS WHERE WE CAN SEE THEM" NOW!! DO IT NOW!!.

All I could hear was shouting & banging whilst I'm upstairs thinking shit my "straps" I'm fucked, there was no way out I was trapped I couldn't do anything but surrender and to be honest, I didn't feel like getting shot. I can't remember if they smashed the door down or maybe my mum let them in, I think she saved them the trouble plus I don't think she would have been best pleased having her front door taken off its hinges early hours of the morning together with armed police pointed firearms in her face.

4–5 armed response police officers wearing goggles & balaclavas holding MP5 machine guns & Glock 17's came rushing upstairs together with the leading investigating officers on the case and arrested me for 6 counts which included 1, attempted murder ×1, 2, possession of a firearm with intent to danger life, 3, possession of a firearm ×2, 4, possession of ammunition without a legal certificate, ×6, 5, prohibited use of a firearm in a public place ×2, 6, possession of a controlled substance meaning cannabis 250 grams in total.

I was escorted to Longsight police station where I was interviewed over the shooting for over 8 hours and replied (NO COMMENT) to all questions put towards me through the course of the interview and while I was in custody at the station the search of my home address resulted in them finding the firearms but at the time they couldn't put them on me without testing them for forensic analysis they also tested me for G.S.R plus took my clothes.

The evidence wasn't concrete enough for them to hold us or remand us in custody so they gave us bail with conditions pending further investigation and to attend back at the station at a later date. The police didn't give a shit because they released us right in the middle of enemy territory we were walking behind enemy lines, luckily we saw a friend that we knew driving past us it was a sign of relief, to be honest, I felt blessed it was good timing. Unknown to us as we pulled Into the street where we were getting dropped off two A.R.V (armed response vehicles) parked up on the side (BELLY) the driver panics and speeds of talking about he's a band driver the police guy on the passenger's side of his jeep points his fingers at me aggressively than sirens start to echo (BELLY) hits couple corners to avoid capture he's got his girlfriend in the front while me and my homie are cramped in the back of this VW POLO and to make matters worse there's a dog with us in the back seat flying around the car because this guy is racing over the humps with speed we hit Kings Road where he let us out on the corner of St Johns Road.

Told him bless for the lift exchange a few words and he was off again with the sirens in the far distance.

I couldn't believe it straight out of the police station and into a hot pursuit with the fifties, just my luck.

Whilst on bail under investigation the C.I.D & murder squad were building their case against us still watching us making it difficult for us to move around, but at this time we had different stolen cars parked up plus motorbikes was a good way to get away from from the police. There was one officer in the hood that always use to hound me even as a kid so when I was under investigation for the shooting he made it his duty to harass me constantly always on my back wanted to stop me all the time proper robocop (P.C ROBOCOP) was his name from the C.I.D department in Stretford. At that time I bought a Mazda Exodus 2.5 V6 on an X reg it was a beauty and one of my favourite cars together with my Nissan Cherry Turbo along with many others I cherished back then.

One evening on a cold winters night in November (P.C ROBOCOP) spotted me behind the wheel of my Mazda Exodus, he gave chase but I lost him through the back street of the Ozone plus my Exodus was a V6 2.5 engine he had no chance it was over before it even started; because he knew it was me plus he knew I was a band driver so he put a warrant out for my arrest so I had most of the police force out in the hood getting about with a printed picture looking for me.

With being on bail for the shooting my days were numbered anyway plus I had the firearms hanging over my head which I thought I might have to plead guilty too because my mum or family wasn't getting the blame plus I knew it was only a matter of time before the forensics came back on the firearms which would have shown .38 revolver being responsible for the shooting.

I was hunted down where they found me hiding in my mums' bedroom took me to Stretford police station and charged me for the band driving plus dangerous driving and obstruction of a police officer from his duties.

I was remanded in custody and later sentenced at Manchester magistrates to a 4 months custodial at (HMP/YOI HINDLEY) where I remained to complete my sentence.

During my temporary stay at (HMP/YOI HINDLEY) one morning, I was in the gym lifting a few weights with a few of the homies when a screw approached me and said I've got a visitor and they've been waiting for a while, in my mind I had no idea I had a prison visit an I wasn't aware of one unless it had been booked an organised by my family which I would know about so this visit was a surprise to me and I was intrigued to know who was awaiting me. I made my way down to the visiting hall where I was greeted by a tall slim white male suited and booted tie slick shoes well dressed and before I could even say anything he responds with

My name is (Mark Twain) I'm from Robert Lizard solicitors nice to meet you I'm your appointed solicitor "Let's waste no time, I'm here to inform and give you an update off your outstanding case which you have 6 serious offences pending & we've been notified by the police that some new damaging information has come to light".

My energy went from high to low very quickly and asked him what's the evidence surrounding the case that's brought him here he replied do you know a woman called (Joanne Telling) I sat there thinking for a few minutes as he pulls out a black folder containing a 4-page statement and begins to read out this new evidence which has been forwarded onto him from the G.M.P and C.P.S (Crown prosecution service).

As he's reading this statement I'm sat there thinking (WTF) has happened within these last few weeks of being locked down it was iffy I could smell a rat he gave me a copy of the evidence which I brought back to my cell and I remember staying up all night going over all the evidence they had against me.

The most damaging was the new piece of evidence the police had received from (Joanne Telling) which she explained and states that we went to her house the morning of the shooting spoke with her son for a while then left basically what I was reading was her placing me my homie at the scene of the shooting, regardless If they think we did or not her statement placing us there around that time together with the .38 revolver that they found and sent off for forensics it wasn't rocket science that they had the right guy and it gave them all the time in the world because I was in custody doing a 4-month sentence.

I was due to be released on the 21st of February 2005 so police knew this date and knew It wasn't long before I was released and back on the street again, February the 12th a week before I'm due to be released from prison the same thing happened I got an unexpected visit this time I'm in the education department when two screws came to collect me and took me to the visits hall, at this time I'm thinking it's my barista or solicitor so I didn't think too much of it.

As I walked into the rooms that were separate from the actual visitation room it was the governor of the prison with an extra few screws behind him I was bemused puzzled confused thinking (WTF) is going on.

I was told to state my name and prison number before being told to be seated my mind still racing to wonder what's about to happen my thoughts of solicitors and baristas immediately left my thinking process when I all heard was the governor say we're taking you down to reception where you will be greeted by the police, I was silent with my brain doing overtime I didn't say a word as the screws escorted me down to reception.

They put me in a holding cell for about ten minutes but through the window, I could see through the gap of the gate where I noticed a police van with another car in front as my minds doing overtime counting the cracks in the ceiling the door cracks open with 2 screws standing there "right feller there ready for ya".

I was escorted to the reception area and greeted by two suit-wearing officers unaware to me that it's murder squad coming to charge me with all of the 6 offences.

I was transported from (HMP/YOI HINDLEY) back to Manchester Longsight police station where I was again under caution and re-arrested and charged with the shooting along with all the rest of the other offences.

I was transported back to prison a few hours later with new charges hanging over me this time it was more serious charges I knew at this point it was game over and the following week I received solicitors Rule 39 correspondence letter that was issued from Manchester Crown Court stating that I am to be remanded into custody and remain in custody and my release date for the 21st of February is no longer effective.

From that moment onwards it was to be the start of a long journey through the prison system. I was made a Category-A high-risk prisoner which I will talk more about in the upcoming chapter of (prison-the concrete grave) a trial date was set for later the following year and I remained in custody until I was found guilty and sentenced to 17 years custody with 7 years running concurrently because of a guilty plea to the firearms before trial.

MRS "BLABBERMOUTH"

Supergrass is a British slang term for an informant who turns queens evidence, often in return for protection and immunity from prosecution. In the British criminal world, police informants have been called "grasses" since the late 1930s, and the "super" prefix was coined by journalists in the early 1970s to describe those who witnessed against fellow criminals in a series of high-profile mass trials at the time. The origin of the term "grass" being used as signifying a traitor, a person who informs on people he or she knows intimately, ostensibly can be traced to the expression "snake in the grass", which has a similar meaning. The phrase derives from the writings of Virgil (in Latin, latet Anguis in herba) and has been known in the English language, meaning "traitor", since the late 17th century.

An alternative claim is made for the term originating from rhyming slang, whereby "grasshopper" is defined as "copper", meaning policeman.

My homies mum ended up coming to court as a witness for the prosecution, after all, the evidence they had was all circumstantial plus it didn't look good with all the gang-related stuff they had against me from building a case around my gang history and criminal record.

I was expecting repercussions for those that snitched no games played but it didn't go down that way and now the betrayal of my so-called people have turned their back on me I was pissed off frustrated angry and could not believe that I protected my people but I was the one who was getting shitted on.

The recent incarnation of the saying is from hip-hop culture, but it originally comes from the gangland or mafia code of "omertá" which dictates silence regarding crimes committed by one's gang. 'Snitches get stitches.

In the world of being on the streets and being involved in the world of crime, you have a code to live by there is rules and regulations it's written in stone from before our time that you don't snitch at all you keep your mouth closed zipped lip.

On the flip side to that coin, some don't live & stick by the code and they end up going out like cowardly people or they do it to save themselves just remember the game don't love you and I certainly realised that when my people told on me and sent me down the way on a 10-year journey through the prison system.

Motive - (JUDGE ANTHONY GEE).

At Manchester Crown Court Judge Anthony Gee said the shot was fired by young Grossman as he and Houghton-Savage, who was armed with the sawn-off shotgun, walked through "Doddington territory".

"I am satisfied the gangland background was the motive behind the shooting.

There is a dangerous rivalry between the gangs but I don't sentence you for membership.

"It seems to me that both of you deliberately armed yourselves with weapons to use them if an opportunity presented itself.

"The carrying and the use of firearms will not be tolerated in any civilised society. The public rightly expects the courts to pass deterrent sentences on offenders involved in such dangerous activities."

THE SENTENCE.

Grossman, from Old Trafford, was given 17 years detention but 7 concurrent after pleading guilty before trial to the firearms and Houghton-Savage, from Chorlton, got nine years after they were cleared of attempted murder but convicted of possessing firearms with intent to endanger life.

Grossman also admitted possessing the revolver when it was found in a bin at his home after the shooting, together with ammunition for a different gun used for a .357 magnum and a Derringer .22 calibre pistol.

THE EFFECTS OF GANG LIFE.

Consequences of gang membership may include exposure to drugs and alcohol, age-inappropriate sexual behaviour, difficulty finding a job because of lack of education and work skills, removal from one family, imprisonment and even death. Through the eyes of the law, many will agree and believe that Gangs increase the levels of crimes in communities, and set a bad example for kids in the area. They create an image of power and respect when in reality they drop out of school, struggle with unemployment, abuse drugs and alcohol or end up in jail. Communities fear them because of the harm they can bring to others. Where in reality that's not all facts because despite how you look at it my community didn't look at me like that probably certain individuals would but that's only the ones that don't know you for who you are as a person so misconceptions and bad characteristics are downfalling for many good people no matter if there gang-related. Family breakdowns, poverty, poor housing, addiction, educational failure, crime, violence and unemployment create the mindset of people wanting to feel loved because it's not all about the "gang" code to many it's about feeling loved and wanted and especially for those that have been raised in poverty and no nothing different because no matter how you look at it the chances for those living, under those circumstances, it's enervating their energy where they feel they have no one so it's understandable for those to want to be around the love, money, cars, clothes, women, you know the most things that come with the street life. My advice for those that don't need to join a gang or be involved with what doesn't concern them is Joining a gang will not give you more protection; it could enhance your chance of being targeted as a victim. Gang members make far less money than those who do not join gangs. Gang members usually don't get a good education, making it hard to find a good job. It's common sense and the outline of what can happen in that gang life because everyone knows right from wrong and it's your choice whether you want to jeopardise your life also your family & freedom. To the many tainted souls that have been raised around it and saw nothing but misery & pain from violence from an early age because of the surroundings they were in it's not, we can just eradicate from our lives and maybe certain things in life ain't the way it's supposed to be but all we can do is keep it pushing and remain real and guide the kids to do something better with their life regardless of we can't change ourselves giving back to the community is always a good deed and in my opinion, it's a deed that will never go unnoticed which shouldn't include any religious beliefs but from the heart of a man that's been there and lived through the experience.

Another thing you have to be careful of is disloyalty from your so-called friends because there's always a few that have agendas, so you have to keep your grass cut to try to avoid the snakes but you can still get bit MEANING that you could know a person for years and still get stabbed in the back. Especially within that gang life, and it's always the people you know that turn on you for many reasons may that be money, girls, or any sort of material processions that you may have it's a vicious circle of jealousy and spite plus there's a lot of very bad mind people.

I say that again for the reader to fully understand my outlook on the effects of one-off the realities of being involved in gang life. Also, the downsides of friendships are the potential for a friend to backstab or betray you, when a friend turns against you it may feel like the end of the world especially if this person is who you would normally turn to during those times of need. Coping with friends who turn against you requires compassionate attention to your own emotions as well as closely considering the status of the current relationship and moving forward accordingly. Learn how to care for your hurt feelings and handle a disloyal friend, too. Plus a few little signs that you can tell that your friends are acting funny.

Signs Your Friends Don't Respect You.

1. They are overly demanding. You are not allowed to have any free time for yourself. ...
2. They are flaky and not in the way we are all a little flaky. ...
3. They belittle you to make themselves seem cooler in front of others. ...
4. They get jealous easily

Plus you get (individual risk) factors such as; History of violent victimization. Furthermore, the more your lifestyle results in the criminal life you can develop;

- Attention deficits, hyperactivity, or learning disorders.
- History of early aggressive behaviour.
- Involvement with drugs, alcohol, or tobacco.
- Low IQ.
- Poor behavioural control.
- Deficits in social cognitive or information-processing abilities.
- High emotional distress.

Those include (protective) factors: Early aggressive behaviour, lack of parental supervision, academic problems, undiagnosed mental health problems, peer substance use, drug availability, poverty, peer rejection, and child abuse or neglect are risk factors associated with increased likelihood of youth substance use and abuse, and many more serious other factors come into play.

- Biological Risk Factors. Just like we can't choose our eye colour, we can't choose the chemical makeup of our brain. ...
- Adverse Childhood Experiences. ...
- Negative Social Environment. ...

Violence triggers were exposure to violence, parental bereavement, self-harm, traumatic brain injury, accidental injury, or substance intoxication. .....

How does violence affect your life?

It causes depression, anxiety and other mental health disorders such as paranoia. It also contributes to cancer, heart disease, stroke and HIV/AIDS because victims of violence often try to cope with their traumatic experiences by adopting risky behaviours such as using tobacco, alcohol and drugs, as well as engaging in unsafe sex. Plus the communities with gang activity are disproportionately affected by theft, negative economic impact, vandalism, assault, gun violence, illegal drug trade, and homicide.

To prevent the youth of today from joining gangs, communities must strengthen families and schools, improve community supervision, train teachers and parents to manage disruptive youth, and teach students interpersonal skills and knowledge not just outcast kids or label them as trouble makers learn to understand where these kids come from understanding their feelings let their voices be heard. Instead of downgrading the youth let's uplift them because the root causes of crime [are] poverty, unemployment, underemployment, racism, poor health care, bad housing, weak schools, mental illness, alcoholism, single-parent families, teenage pregnancy, and a society of selfishness and greed. So if we can teach the young from early it prevents having to cure later on in life we need to make sure that the knowledge and wisdom are passed on to the next generation of youths.

As my chapter of gang life comes to a close I would like to take this time out to give (YOU) the reader a big thank you for being part of this journey with me.

I would like to say I can't talk too much about my involvement in gang activity as I don't want to incriminate myself or others, plus I can only talk about my crimes that are already documented and the way the gang life affected me and shaped my world.

On the other hand, there are many people I have a lot of respect for within the life of crime and gangs, some bad some good and some I'd rather not think about, but in all my time spent around the influences of gang life I can say that it taught me many things but the most important lessons of all were about the people we surround ourselves with and it's not all flashy cars diamonds rings & big gold chains nice watches and sexy girl's there's a dark side to gang life a wicked side.

One thing that you do need to grasp is the fact that just because you may have a lot of people around you, don't mean those people are going to be there for you when shit gets real, but you only realise when it's too late and that's what happens most of the time whereas If you could just see what you couldn't see before maybe you would think twice about joining or hanging around people that you know is bad influences also the energy is not good for you.

But on the flip side, we all go through life as a lesson so therefore it's for yourself to learn from mistakes and from observing others on how they went wrong so you can obtain the knowledge and make progress without continuously making the same mistakes as they did.

With much respect for the families of many that have lost their loved ones due to gang-related violence my heart still bleeds and continues to do so m, I have faith that one day your life will be filled with happiness despite the hurt you carry most days.

To all the people across the nation that are suffering from everyday violence daily from the prisons, schools, communities, family homes, domestic relationships may the wounded heal and in time hopefully, it gets better because at the end of the day it's the children that suffer and I'm not one to preach or be a hypocritical person but the consequences of our ignorance and gang activities have a damaging impact on the children.

If I had to give advice but not be a hypocrite I would say stay in school kids educate yourself you'll live a better life in the long run listen to your peers family and good friends those with good hearts and don't be so quick to grow upkeep your innocents and keep it away as far as possible from any negative people or situations stay humble.

REST IN PEACE TO ALL THE PEOPLE, LOVED ONE'S FAMILY & FRIENDS AND THOSE THAT HAVE SADLY LOST THEIR LIVES NOT ONLY TO GUN CRIME BUT JUST IN LIFE, MAY THE GOOD SPIRITS PROTECT THE SOULS OF THEIR LOVED ONES THAT CONTINUOUSLY GO THROUGH THE PAIN OF NOT BEING ABLE TO LIVE LIFE WITH THEIR FALLEN ANGELS, MAY THE GOOD SPIRITS LEAD THEM ON THE RIGHTEOUS PATH OF HAPPINESS AND CONTINUE TO GUIDE & PROTECT THEM FROM EVIL.

Signed Aaron Nathan Grossman.
(AKA Locz Da Sixth)

Left to right:
Aaron, Lance
Houghton-Savage,
JJ Fletcherman
and Omar
Berryman

Lee Amos and
Colin Joyce

Aaron

Mandem
in the '90's

Zico Reid at the top. Joel Gordon left, Wesley Blackett middle and Fabian Ricketts far right.

CHAPTER EIGHT

Prison.
The Concrete Grave.
From A - D.

When someone arrives at the prison system they have at least one interview and assessment with a qualified professional so they:

- know what their rights are.
- get help with their physical and mental health, for example with sexual health or drug and alcohol problems.
- are told what courses they can do in prison.
- understand prison rules and procedures.

The prisoner gets a prisoner number and their property is recorded and put somewhere safe until they're released.

Hindley Prison opened in 1961 as a Borstal in 1983 it was re-classified as a Youth Custody Centre. Hindley was then re-classified as an adult prison and in 1997 it became a joint prison and Young Offenders Institution.

In 2015 Hindley was reclassified as a full adult jail for offenders over the age of 21.

In 2002, when I was there Her majesty's chief inspectors of Prisons recorded many good initiatives taking place at Hindley, particularly in suicide prevention, drugs strategy, sentence planning and joint work with the police service to monitor and act on racial incidents. However, the Inspector criticised inadequate reception procedures, insufficient purposeful activity and patchy help with resettlement at the prison.

In December 2004 a security alert was sparked when two inmates staged a roof-top protest at Hindley Prison.

More than 100 extra staff were drafted in to deal with a riot at the prison on 5th October 2005. It took more than seven weeks to fully restore the prison wing after the riot which caused more than £145,000 damage. I left 8-9 months before double cuffed on a Cat-A bus heading down the M25 to Buckinghamshire before this event which was brewing long before I even left that establishment.

Hindley is a Young Offender Institution, near Wigan, which holds both young adults (18-21) and juveniles (15-18) before its reclassification in 2015 to just housing adults.

As in all the split sites that the H.M.C.I.O.P (Her majesty's chief inspector of Prisons) inspect, there is a marked discrepancy in provision for the two groups. Juveniles, who have only been held at Hindley since July 2001, were housed in newer accommodation and benefit from much greater financial investment, through separate funding from the Youth Justice Board. This is an invidious disparity, which runs through the whole prison system. Split sites demonstrate this most acutely. But they also provide an opportunity to share the learning, if not the resources, acquired with juveniles, to drive up standards for all young people in custody. For this reason, in 2003 an inspection was carried out by a combined team of inspectors from the prisons young prisoner and juvenile teams, whose analysis and recommendations are set out in their reports.

Fundamentally, Hindley provided a safe environment for the young people in its care. Both juveniles and young adults were treated well in reception despite the long delays and the potentially traumatic first night was managed with care and sensitivity not for all though that has to be said.

Suicide and self-harm procedures were among the best they had seen, owned by the whole prison and with clear senior management support: indeed they described them as a model of good practice. However, by contrast, measures to detect and prevent bullying, both among juveniles and young adults, were deficient. As a consequence, significantly more young people than at the time of the last inspection held that information gained from prison authorities told them that young adults believed to being victimised by other young prisoners, and more felt unsafe. Besides, the governor was rightly keeping under scrutiny the high rates of use of force; and specifically the appropriateness of Prison Service control and restraint techniques, designed for use on adults rather than young people.

Staff–prisoner relationships were generally good, although there were deficiencies in both the systems and environment needed to support and develop mutual respect, particularly in the case of young adults.

The personal officer scheme, on both sides of the establishment, required development, as did the applications system as you would put in an application and wouldn't receive it back for like 7-10 days when it should have been 3-5 working days plus the race relations work needed to be strengthened. Young people were also vociferous in their condemnation of the quality and quantity of food and the quality of prison-issue clothing and bedding, and they agreed.

Finally, there was a stark contrast between the grubby and impoverished accommodation of the young adults and that of the juveniles.

There was an impressive amount of purposeful activity at Hindley I have to say, with full employment and extensive access to music courses within the education department. This was particularly the case on the juvenile side that I was on; but it was commendable that, despite the differential in resources, they found only 39 out of 320 young adults unoccupied during the core day. Accredited training was only just being introduced and needed to expand, but education provision was largely very good: though once again better on the juvenile side I was on.

The one serious omission was the inadequate opportunity to spend time in the open air one hour of exercise per day was provided but not all the time especially if there was a lockdown.

Resettlement was an area that had received considerable management attention and the results were impressive. Sentence planning for young adults and training planning for juveniles were effective; there was a range of offending behaviour programmes, a clear and focused drug strategy and several other resettlement projects. However, there was the need for greater coordination, based upon a needs analysis, and there were also some gaps in provision: for example, the lack of treatment for juvenile sex offenders, which they say needs to be addressed both locally whereas I see that as nationally syndicated by government tyranny.

Overall, they said it was a largely positive inspection report in 2003/2004 of an establishment that was seeking to maximise purposeful activity and had made a good start on resettlement.

While Hindley was generally safe, managers needed to give the same attention and focus to anti-bullying work as they had to the prevention of suicide and self-harm: as both are essential parts of a safer prison environment. They were, however, aware of this deficit, as they were of many of the others that inspectors brought to their attention; and they say they were actively working to overcome that deficit but in a slow process.

However, they were still faced with the disparity in investment in young adults as compared to juveniles. Such relative deprivation on a split site is difficult to justify, not least to the young people themselves; but it is now, sadly, an all too familiar feature of the prison system.

The Youth Justice Board announced on 23 October 2014 that it will be withdrawing completely from Hindley. Hindley Prison is no longer a youth offender prison.

It holds Category-C male prisoners from the age of 18 upwards.

Accommodation at the prison is made up of seven secure units, consisting of single and double cells.

Hindley is a combined establishment with a regime that offers opportunities for inmates to gain qualifications, address offending behaviour, and reintegrate back into society on their release.

Regime provision includes learning and skills, as well as workshop places (which include construction skills) and physical education program's.

Hindley also operates a listener and peer support scheme for those who may be at risk of suicidal tendencies or self-harm The prison's medical provision includes an in-patient healthcare facility and a mental health day-care centre.

I landed in (HMP/YOI HINDLEY) on May 13th 2003 originally sentenced to four months do half for a street robbery I committed by myself one afternoon walking just patrolling the hood.

I noticed this guy on the opposite side of the road with his earphones in just going about his day minding his own business I approached him he was average in size slim build with ginger scuffed hair with a little stubble beard looking like a hippie.

I asked if he a cigarette which he didn't hear because of the music he was pumping through the earphones I shouted (YO) as he saw I was talking to him adjusting the wires that were tangled in his coat. I replied again with a more aggressively louder tone

"(U GOT A PIECE OF CIG FOR ME)" he responded that he didn't smoke (ME) on the other hand made it an excuse that he replied in an aggressive tone and he was to apologise for the way he was speaking which he replied (IM SORRY MATE IM JUST TRYING TO GET TO WORK).

I didn't care at that point because all I was thinking about was his earphones I don't know why because

I didn't have any device to use them with and they had absolutely no relevance whatsoever to my life. He walked off at a quicker pace than he was originally walking I think he probably had the thought of getting robbed and possibly beaten up for his belongings so I sped up behind him grabbing him from behind in a chokehold type position he reacted kindly swiftly his reflexes were on point so a struggle broke out live on the main road it's surprising thinking back that no cars stopped because it did look like we were fighting but in actuality it was me trying to jack him for his shit. I got the better of him as he started to scream and shout "help help help" I made off with his phone and wallet not realising there's a taxi man sat In his car that witnessed the incident.

I hit the alleyway after hearing car tyres screeching from behind me plus a car door opening with the voice shouting in the background "OII YOU" without even looking back I was on my toes throwing bins down making the alleyway like an obstacle course in his path and more difficult for him to catch an keep up with me. I was too quick for him and took off down the alleys like a greyhound chasing a hare.

I didn't hesitate on selling the Nokia 3310 and stolen credit cards to the Asians on Wilmslow road, at the of back the shops we new an Asian guy that would buy all sorts of electronic products and items of everyone & anyone phones and cards is all we used to take to him regardless of it being stolen or not even if the people reported it and got it blocked he would buy it because he used to send them back to his homeland of Pakistan.

I got arrested for that offence a few days later standing outside the shops and got spotted by police with the victim in the back seat pointing me out like an I.d parade I tried to abscond but got blocked in after a short pursuit, I got charged and sent to the juvenile courts and ended up with probation and tag with a curfew time of 7 till 7 that I had to stick to for 4 months but I used to take it off and stick it on my sister's ankle and let her wear it because it detects when you left the house after curfew hours and sometimes the police would end up coming to check that you're indoors and if you weren't you'd get locked up for violation of your license conditions.

I originally had been sentenced to attend the (Y.O.T) part of Probation a period during which a person who has committed a crime has to obey the law and be supervised by a probation officer, rather than being sent to prison.

Whilst on probation after getting sentenced for the street robbery my good friend (C-Loc) that I was with one day had seen the same guy that I robbed previously seeing him again made sense that he must have lived in the same area we chilled out but this time he was standing at the bus stop with another guy he looked a few years older than me and (C-Loc) due to his body mass and size.

He immediately recognised me as we locked eyes and I could see the fear because don't forget he's already got me locked up once before now I'm on probation for the robbery the last thing I need to be doing is getting involved in another charge especially on the same boy but me being me I just couldn't help it and ran over and just punched the kid straight in the face (C-Loc) straight away pounced on the other guy kicking punching swearing calling him a dirty little snitch a few civilians that had been walking past saw what was going on and thought it was just a fight between four lads but it was us kicking the shit out off these boys another couple that was walking intervened and broke it up which then gave the boys a chance to run away we were in hot pursuit after them but they ran into a shop for protection.

Not even 48 hours later "BANG BANG" first thing in the morning police banging down my mum's door I could see yellow coats through the glass of my front door and before I knew it 6-7 officers storming the hallway of my house and I knew exactly what was going on "BOOM" they charged into my room and arrested me for assault and causing distress to the public which made me look even worse when it came to court for sentencing but the pre-sentence reports from probation helped me a little bit because I had a good reference from certain public figures that I knew in the community and the probation guy that was assigned to work with me made out I was just a lost teenager that needed a bit off guidance but still they revoked the original sentence because of my breeches and gave me my first-ever prison sentence of four months in (HMP/YOI HINDLEY) a well-known detention centre.

On the way to (HMP/YOI HINDLEY) from getting slammed at the courts which we referred to as magistrates "SALE NO BAIL" even though the crime committed was in Rusholme Manchester a mile down the road from my home town of Old Trafford being a residence still living under my mums' roof they moved the case to Sale, in Trafford otherwise the case would off been heard at the Manchester magistrates youth courts in Manchester town centre.

I already had a few homies there at HINDLEY when I landed so I was okay for accessories like shower gels, phone cards, munchies, music, weed you name it I could get it or I knew a man who knew a man who could get anything you wanted.

(It's not what you know in prison it's who you know in prison and what respect you have your credentials and how you carry yourself)

When people think of prison they automatically think all kinda weird stuff and their mind wanders and gets tangled with the negative effects of the mind playing tricks on you especially with all the prison documentary's that you may off watched the thought can be a very daunting task, to say the least never mind being behind those walls and bars.

I was fifteen years old taking my first steps entering through the gates of prison life. It's not like it's been something that I've not been used to having my liberty taken away in some sort of way, I never liked authorities from being young whether that was teachers or police or any kind of figure that wanted to impose their authority on me so the prison officers known as (SCREWS) the English terminology of a prison officer came under that same umbrella.

The actual term (SCREW) originally screwed as a term for a prison guard is based on the fact that screw was origi- nally slang for "key." One of the most important functions of a prison guard, or turnkey, as he's often called, is to see that prisoners are locked up at the appropriate times – and that involves turning the "screw." Interestingly enough, ... that's just a few facts that I discovered chatting to a few older heads or even certain prison officials like governors that want to give you their knowledge because he would off been in the system for over 20+ years.

My sentence was only four months do half so my stay at (HMP/YOI HINDLEY) was shit and a shave as they say behind those walls. I landed on F-Wing where there were only a few of my homies that I knew from the street loads off scousers but all my closest homies that I grew up with was literally to the side of me on E-Wing.

I stayed on F-Wing for 2-3 weeks before I put in a trans- fer for a wing change to be with my closest but before

I even got to move I had to go through some risk assessments because security within the jail was concerned that If more of our homies were together that we would be more difficult to control and monitor.

That process took around a week before I got the green light that I could move I was happy to be around my people for my last six weeks or so plus they had access to more things like weed, phones & homemade alcohol that was known as (HOOCH). Before I eventually moved all the time I'd have to go to the gym, chapel or education to meet up with my people to get my shit so moving with them and having access to the stuff I needed without having to wait for it was good for me and worked out in my favour.

The food wasn't the best but there were only certain days that the food wasn't too bad it was edible but not what you'd expect to eat outside being at home I soon found out that this place certainly wasn't an ain't no five-star hotel restaurant.

I ate noodles and tuna which became one of the best combinations you could eat and you could eat that any time of the day and best believe me you did get hungry very hungry so if you weren't doing a little hustle on the backhand or you didn't have family support you was kind off existing but not living. Porridge with warm milk was a good source of protein especially in the mornings and afternoons but the milk was in a small carton you had to rip the label type sticker of the milk to just have the cardboard underneath throw that in the bowl of boiling water from the hot water dispenser that was on the wing leave that to settle for like 5 minutes with something over the top to keep the heat from exiting.

That's not just me having to survive on prison tactics of survival because In all English prisons each prisoner receives a breakfast pack which is issued the evening before for use the next morning. This will include a bowl of breakfast cereal, milk, tea bags, coffee whitener, sugar, brown or white bread, jam and margarine or butter type spread and you're telling me you can live off that one carton when you might want to make a hot beverage or something that requires you to need milk it was hard enough milk was like gold to get sometimes unless you bought it off the canteen courtesy of (UHT) production.

Not often on the menu these days

According to the prison rules, all prisoners are supposed to receive three meals a day, of which at least one must include the option of hot food.

Most nicks have abandoned any pretence of serving breakfast as a specific timetabled meal. Instead, inmates get issued with what is very grandly called a 'breakfast pack'.

These are pretty much standardised across the prison estate and consist of a clear plastic bag containing four loose tea bags, four small sugar sachets, four packets of whitener and a tiny bag of cereal, muesli or porridge oats. Most closed nicks also provide a 0.25 one carton of semi-skimmed milk, although if you're unlucky the porridge oats will have had a sachet of whitener put in it already and then you don't get any milk.

There's still a few "nicks" in the English prison term for those who don't know: that still provide hot toast in the morning, but out of the six jails I've been in, only 2 out 6 still did so. There is still a D-cat (open) prison in England that continues to provide a full cooked breakfast seven days a week. There is hot porridge on offer at the servery hotplate, as well as eggs served in various ways, plus sausage and either beans or tomatoes. It's pretty good, too I was shocked.

Moreover, if you are expecting inmates to do hard physical labour in the fields and farmyards from morning until evening – the animals have to be fed etc – then you can't feed them a small bag of cereal. Most other prisons have ditched the idea of self-sufficiency, so there isn't much hard physical labour still available in the nick. Breaking rocks went out of fashion about 60 years ago.

The midday meal in most prisons now consists of a pre-ordered sandwich or 'baguette' (no relation to the tasty French bread of the same name), sometimes with soup as an additional offering, but often not.

Tea (served around 5.30 pm in many nicks) is usually the main meal of the day, although at weekends some nicks serve the sandwich in the afternoon, with the lunch-time offering being cooked. In theory, this is supposed to be hot food, although salad options are often available.

These meals range from pretty good, to truly inedible. Often the catch is inconsistency. One week, the shepherd's pie will be very good, the following week it will taste as if one of the shepherds has contributed his oldest pair of sweaty socks to the ingredients. You could liken it to playing culinary Russian roulette.

Obviously like I said if your not clued up and don't adapt to the way of prison life your time will be hard so to make it better for myself even though I did have support from the outside that wasn't enough because my mum at that time couldn't afford to send me money all the time £10 £15 minimum had to last me for two weeks an education was only good for the art & technology & graphic design.

Depending on where you were all prisoners can earn? Minimum rates of pay are laid down by the Prison Service, although the actual rates vary according to individual jails and the kind of job they are doing or the course they are taking in educational programs.

Although the minimum rate is £4, the average weekly pay is £9.60 but in some occupations like working in the prison kitchen inmates can earn up to £20+.

That's mostly in the area of departments like Education and work. All residents have access to education and training provided depending on what educational services the prison establishment comes under. Residents can work on their literacy and numeracy before progressing to work-related training in catering and hospitality, multi-media, construction, distribution and warehousing, or community development.

Residents can also study for a wide range of professional sports qualifications.

Residents can work in a range of roles in prison and the best job in my opinion especially the trusted ones are the kitchen, gym, chapel, library, gardens, waste centre and stores but most require a risk assessment management process.

One funny morning I remember getting nicked which is placed on the governors report when (D.S.T) dedicated search team raided my cell and found pornographic magazines.

We couldn't buy them or get them sent in because we were under the age of eighteen so only the adults could receive them but I had my connections my homeboy was over there and we got to see each other passing once a week when he came over to the gym on the juvenile side where I was.

It's a funny story actually because I ended up booking up into and chatting to my homeboy actually in the segregation unit the following morning told him what had happened and why I was down there he immediately started laughing he was joking about it for a bit then he said "don't worry they can have it try to get to my cell door before you go back" I was like "ok" cool with a little smirk laugh as the conversation turned to laughter between us together with the sound of keys outside my cell the door cracks open it was 2 screws stood there one with a musty type beard grey-haired while the other was a bigger build like he took steroids looking like a proper skinhead racist National.

I was lead to the governours office and before being able to be seated I was told to stand in front of him and was told to issue my name and prison number I responded ("GROSSMAN-DH6715") at that moment I felt like I wasn't even in prison but in some army boot camp getting disciplined.

He began reading out the charge for owning what they called an "illegal requirement" in other words they classified it as "contraband" don't know why it sounds pathetic but I pleaded guilty to the charge and was in there no longer than 10 15 minutes was hanged my punishment paperwork a sent back to wait in the holding cell in the segregation before returning to the wing.

I was underage so the governor couldn't give me segregated time but I could see in his eyes that he wouldn't off hesitated to give me a few days of solitary confinement he just had that look instead he only gave me loss of earnings at 50% which was half my wages deducted from my canteen loss of TV for a week plus no associating with other inmates for a week which means I'm banged up almost 23 hours a day.

The funny side to that story what I mentioned is that when I was waiting in the holding cell to go back to the wing I couldn't get to my homeboy's cell because of the tight security and watchful eyes of the screws but the cleaner was allowed to walk free and go to peoples cells so my homie shouts me "YO" I replied "YO G" he responds I've sent you some girls to keep you company "don't say I never give you nothing" I laugh and chuckle as a noise off this magazine slides under my cell door open it as it's folded into two magazines looking like they've been around the prison a hundred times, I laugh and reply ("YEA G GOT THAT") I put them down my pants at the side of my leg and walk back to the wing and yea I did share "lol".

(HINDLEY) back then the juveniles didn't have an exercise yard so if you were on loss off privileges getting out of your cell was considered just for showers, phone calls, the rest of the hours was you staring at the bars and trying to look out of the tight small window which had a flap on the door which made it difficult to see so anyone walking past was my assistance to keep the flap open so I could see what was going on the wing. In reality, it's all mind games because you think your missing shit from not being out there mixing and congregating with others but you ain't it's just a bunch of noise the sound of pool balls knocking together with ping pong balls people shouting the bell might sound from a little punch up from time to time but that's just prison life.

I used to hate that because soon as the alarm goes and a fight breaks out everybody has to go behind their doors whether you just getting in the shower regardless of whether you been waiting all day to being in the middle of a phone call in deep conversation with a family and they'll cut the phones off or water to the showers so the two that are fighting would spoil it for everyone that was big hate of mine it did use to piss me off or when punks used to blow the electricity the whole landed would normally go and you'd have to wait till the next day for the screws to put it back on again.

A couple of my closest had to do quite a bit of porridge ranging from 5–7 years so being with them was good for the spirit just to spend some time with them because even before I landed when I was on the other side of the fence I felt it for them so being able to spend a few months together was worth a great deal to me. Time didn't seem to go slow because before I knew it I was 6–7 weeks into my sentence time had flown by too quick from being sentenced in may when I first landed on the bus to the middle of June when I was due to be released well June 13th to be exact.

Funnily enough, I spent my 16th birthday in prison on June 6th and was released a week after would you believe it on Friday the 13th just my luck and I took that suspiciously as I am a very deep thinker and I couldn't help hearing the sarcasm from the screws as I was walking out the gate that I'd be back and they'll see me soon. I responded with a finger and gave them a dirty look as I awaited my release papers to sign and if looks could kill at that moment in time I think I would off been facing a murder charge. Because of my attitude towards the reception staff because of their sarcastic sarcasm, they chose to delay my release normally the release procedure: Each day at 7.45 am, cell doors are unlocked. The prisoners will then get ready for their daily activities, which start at 8.30 am.

Those leaving the prison that morning will be unlocked earlier, at 7.30 am.

I didn't get released till about 10 am that morning but I didn't care because I had a mate that I knew from the street and he was getting out that morning too so I had company sitting in boring reception. I still was pissed off because I had arranged for my people to pick me up that day and ("REDZ") with another called (MALLY) a Jamaican guy that was from our section was outside the prison waiting for me and wasn't to know what was going on with me inside.

I eventually signed my release papers got my property and was handed £43 for travel fees and was released.

I gave my friend (KYLE) that I knew from the street a lift back to the hood because he lived not too far from me and we were heading in the same direction otherwise he would off been getting public transportation and that's just not cool plus I know he would off done the same thing for me so he had to have a seat in the car. Before I hopped in the car I used one of the pound coins at the payphone to phone my mum because I don't think anyone had a mobile phone at the time.

I told her I was out and that I was on my way home.

I was presented with a big pre-rolled spliff to light in the back of the car I hit it a few times then felt my head rush after not having a spliff for a couple of weeks or so immediately after a few hits I felt at ease calm and couldn't wait to get home whilst breathing the nice fresh air that smelt so much nicer plus the air smelt cleaner than being locked in a confined space with very little air conditioning and those ridiculously small ventilation windows in your cell it was good to finally be free.

Exactly one year after my release date in June 2003, I was remanded into custody after already serving a 4 months custodial sentence for driving offences, the gang-related shooting took place while I was outside in the Moss Side area of Manchester.

Well, the gang-related incident happened which left a prominent gang rival seriously injured with a gunshot wound to his head luckily he survived the .38 slug that entered his cranium but unfortunately lost the sight out of his right eye.

I was already doing a custodial sentence for dangerous driving plus failing to stop for police in hot pursuit in the Old Trafford area I wasn't allowed to drive as the judge put a lifetime ban on me so I couldn't drive anything ranging from scooters to motorcycles practically anything with an engine I couldn't drive, because the judge put a marker on my file (NOT TO DRIVE) until passing the extended driving test due to all the joyriding as a youngster.

It's 2004 I find myself back in HMP HINDLEY my next-door neighbour Jamie Fitzgerald is serving a 5-year sentence for burglary and escaping lawful custody.

I was with Jamie in a residential halfway house for children under the care of social services back in the early 2000s, We also went to school together at Egerton High and he was one of many kids like me that was on the rooftops throwing slates at the teachers and the police.

The month of February is fast approaching and I've already been rearrested for 6 counts of various other charges ranging from attempted murder to possession of firearms in a public place without a certificate, possession of a firearm ×2 with a threat to cause fear and violence, possession .357 rounds of ammunition without a license ×6 plus a few other drug-related offences which didn't make it on the indictment and my original release date of February 21st, 2005 has now been abolished.

I felt trapped, I was in an unpleasant situation in which I had a lack of freedom my liberty was taken and all I wanted to do was escape from it but it was only the beginning of a long journey ahead of me through the prison system.

I couldn't sleep for weeks stress was building up causing me to be angry and aggressive towards the screws and inmates, the sleeping arrangements were poor though plus it was in the middle of winter and the mattresses were rock hard just like sleeping on a concrete slab the pillows were rock-solid like as a house brick. In other words the mattresses they provided and pillows are not designed to be comfortable. They are designed to be secure, i.e. hard to hide contraband in. That means the mattresses and pillows are thin with little padding.

The Jail was cold, even in the summer, but the yellow blankets are also often thin and may itch you like hell. However, things like shower shoes, sneakers, soap, deodorant, shampoo and a razor, are all pretty easy to get from someone until you have a chance to buy yours from the canteen you have to Keep your prison ID with you at all times and memorize your inmate number before surrender.

My prison number was (DH6715). Returning one year later they gave me my old prison number what I had previously on my original sentence of 4 months it had only been about one year since I walked out the gates of (HMP/YOI HINDLEY) and I was back this time facing more serious charges.

Now on remand facing more serious charges and a long time thinking and debating whether am going to beat this case, the frustration of being grassed on with the new evidence my emotional state of mind wasn't too good.

Jamie and I talked and communicated about my case to see if there were any areas of the case that could help my defence, my co-defendant was still outside on bail for the charges but ended up getting arrested for driving then got remanded into custody and went to (HMP FOREST BANK).

I stayed in HINDLEY for about 2-3 months after my release was supposed to be the 21st of February, to pass the time there was education, gym, sports, and several different types of educational opportunities with courses for you to get involved in.

I had a visit booked that I forgot I had as I looked on the visitor's list for the day ahead, my Sisters baby's father, BOBBY comes to see me. We rap for about two hours before the visit ends give our respects to each other and he blesses me with an 8th of top-grade weed I slide it in my waist observing keeping a watchful eye on the screws feeling good that I'm going back to my cell to get high because it had been a while since id smoked a spliff and I was gagging for one.

I got back to my cell and couldn't wait to get through the door to roll a fat spliff especially because he put some fresh king size blue rizla in there too I couldn't wait to get my smoke on, I blazed out the cell that looked like a smoke box or a gas chamber. Suddenly the door pops open with a screw standing there instantly recognised the smell and says bloody hell (Grossman) it's like an Amsterdam cafeteria in here, put that out the governor wants you.

Eyes bloodshot red from the Sativa I was just inhaling and smelling of fresh haze I walk with the screw in tow down the landing to the governor's office, state your name and number for the governor (DH6715) (GROSSMAN) Governor- ok please be seated.

The purpose of this meeting is to inform you that we have just had instructions from the home office that your security prison category status has been changed and I am now a Category-A prisoner.

I was bemused and kind of lost because of all these big professional words he was using I didn't understand a word he was saying apart from that my security status has changed but still at this point what he had said means nothing to me it went in one ear and out the window that was behind him, he explained and went through what would happen from thereon.

That night when everyone was behind their doors I was made to hand over all of my belongings to the screws and put them in a blue box what didn't fit had to be thrown away or given to somebody because I could only take what fitted inside the box nothing else, there were no exceptions.

They took everything from my clothes to my cutlery & just left me with plastic bowls and dinner plates everything else was stripped from my cell.

It felt like just another day as I awake with sleep still in the corner of my eyes, waking up in a concrete grave seeing the brown metal bars and feeling cold with the light coming through my cracked windows was an everyday occurrence for me. This day felt like no other literally with me waking up most days before the doors crack open for breakfast, or lunch it was a routine of mine being ready just in case you get rolled on unexpectedly in the morning because that's when you are at your most vulnerable and more likely to get attacked so I liked to be ready in the mornings it became a religious belief for me. Even though the morning felt like no other it was like a cloud of negative thoughts was hovering over me that morning, I felt a little uneasy about the day ahead but didn't take it seriously enough until I realised that my door wasn't getting opened and everybody else was on the landing doing their morning routine.

A few of the good friends on the wing noticed that my door wasn't open and came to my cell and asked me what was going on he thought I'd done something wrong but even I had no idea what was happening to me, I got on my buzzer and called for a screw to ask what was going on why was my door not open for breakfast, few minutes had passed when the officer showed up at my door and told me I have to stay behind my door until the governor comes and speaks to me and he can't tell me anymore.

The call for labour and education echoes throughout landed and everybody starts making their way of the wing to their designated workshops and classes and I'm still not sure what the governor wants to speak to me for.

Everybody has left and it's only me on the wing when my door flys open with 5 screws and the governor standing there with cuffs and a blue & yellow all In one type jumpsuit, it smelled musty and was something that I've never seen before in the prison system this clobber was something new to me.

Before I knew it I was double cuffed in walking distance from reception and being placed in a holding cell waiting for additional information about the future of my life in the prison system, I was in reception no longer than 10 minutes before seeing the prison nurse practitioner making sure I was fit and well.

Few papers that I had to sign about my well-being and then the nurse was out the door keys swinging making that irritating jingling sound, in the distance, I could hear voices but remain clueless about what they're talking about loud voices with laughter from the screws & reception cleaners in the background.

The window was a bit high from the floor so I had to stand on the pipes to get a better view otherwise it was a hard task because at 16 17 years old I was smaller than most people my age they didn't call me Lil-A for anything.

Nothing could prepare me for what was about to happen even if I had a dream about my future prison experience before it was about to commence I would off thought that I'd wake up sweating from a nightmare, but not this time this was real life no dream or nightmares here, just cuffs a banana suit and a category-A prison van with flashing blue lights.

I hopped on the van afro wild looking like one of the Jackson 5 brothers wrists feeling tight because they were double cuffed I noticed I was accompanied by completely different screws from where I've just left and what I'm used to their accents stood out to me straight away the hint of cocky slang but not too strong but just enough for me to recognise they ain't from around here, in fact, they were quite funny and was having a laugh with me wasn't making me feel weird or uncomfortable gave me hot tea and a few beverages, the travel was ok but a very long drive it lasted approximately about 3 hours 45 minutes my ass was surely getting sore especially sat in that tight box on those hard prison van seats with little cushioning.

The radio was continuously playing the same songs over and over again it got to the point where I had to tell the Govs to turn the radio down very low because it's doing my head in, most of the officers were alright, but there was just one that was being a bit awkward for no reason making it difficult taking the piss really but I wasn't to bothered.

As we drove for what felt like an eternity I was bored shitless just reading the road signs on the motorway intrigued trying to get an idea of where I was going even though I had a good sense of direction and I could tell I was heading towards Buckinghamshire down the M25 as well as recognising the voices of the screws,

I can't remember the moment I pulled up to the prison gates but I just remembered stopping after driving for so long my ass was numb like it had fallen asleep and my throat was on fire dry like the Sahara desert, I looked at the sign outside the prison and it was called (HMP WOODHILL) a well-known male adult category-A prison that houses some off Englands most dangerous offenders from killers, rapist, terrorist political prisoners at this point, I didn't know anything about the prison until getting there and doing my research for myself.

(HMP WOODHILL)
(CATEGORY-A THE DUNGEON)

HM Prison Woodhill is a Category A male prison, located in Milton Keynes, England. Woodhill Prison is operated by Her Majesty's Prison Service.

A section of the prison is designated as a Young Offenders Institution. A Secure Training Centre is located next to the prison.

I hopped off the van double cuffed wearing a banana suit that made you stand out like a sore thumb and was escorted to the reception area to get processed by the escorting officers, soon as I walked through the doors of my new home I could tell the difference straight away the atmosphere was more intense I knew than I was in a more secure reformatory the walls the barbed wire everything just hit me differently.

The padlocked cuffed was released from my wrists and it felt so much nicer having my hands freely available to move how I wanted to plus there were red scrape marks from the cuffs and the wrist bone was very uncomfortable with little mobility, I was escorted to a small room where I was stripped from my banana suit searched and told to change into another set of jail clothes. I wasn't scared of entering a maximum-security prison that generally holds prisoners serving long sentences. Plus these prisoners ain't your average shoplifters these are people that have committed murder, robbery, kidnapping, treason, or over serious crimes. High stone walls are what I recognised straight away plus those strong barb-wired fences surrounding the perimeter of the most maximum-security establishment. In the United Kingdom, prisoners are divided into four categories of security which I discovered after being upgraded to a different level of category, every adult in prison is assigned a different category, all depending on the crime they committed, the sentence, the risk of escape, and violent tendencies.

The higher the category, the worse the convictions are. After getting processed in the reception I had to wait to be assigned a location but I was told by the screws that I would be going down to the segregation unit where id be staying and that would be my new home for the foreseeable future, in my mind I was thinking "the block" "why" but then the officer started to explain the reasons me going down to the segregation unit.

He gave me the rundown of the situation I was in told me I was "starred up" which meant too young to be placed on the wing with adults so I had to be separated from the category-A adults he provided me with some paperwork information clarifying my category status and offered me some knowledge on how things function and how you can make your stay a stress free one, the whole process was something different the blue boxes with all my property in got a full search and x-ray I was made to squat cough and show underneath my balls for any bladed articles or contraband I was an angry young man I felt violated that's when I knew I was in adults jail.

I waited in a holding cell waiting to be transferred from reception to the segregation unit, I didn't realise that I was placed in a coloured holding cell that allocates your category so the local inmates coming from the courthouse had to walk past me and was asking me why am I in the yellow holding cell.

I didn't know what they were talking about until one of the inmates was explaining about the coloured cells the one I was in was for category-A prisoners the blue one was for sex offenders & V.P's (Vulnerable Prisoner) and the red one was for the general public court's normal locations etc, I shouted through the vent holes of the cell door that I was category-A and I've just been transferred from (HPM/YOI HINDLEY) they asked how old I was which I replied I was 17 years old they asked me about my offence and why I was category-A so I told them in conversation about my shooting and firearm offences and that I was from Manchester they started to laugh and say I was a crazy youngster.

The sound of keys and footsteps was approaching my cell; as the keys enter the keyhole a different officer was standing there with my folder "right feller" as the screw opened his mouth grab your stuff and follow me and stay behind the red zone which was a red line that you had stay behind, I grabbed my belongings and put them in the cart that had four-wheels like a trolley so I didn't have to carry all my property by hand as I came out of the reception doors and was faced with a mean-looking alsatian dog showing it's sharp razor teeth I halted for a split second when the officer said he's the dog handler you can't go anywhere without the dog handler being present and he's here to escort me to the segregation unit without no trouble. I gave a nervous laugh and replied "well I won't be messing around with this dog I'm easy I'm not in the mood to get bitten by an angry canine now or any other time no thanks", he chuckled and replied, "you'll be surprised what people do knowing that there are canines ready to clamp their jaws on some flesh" personally I didn't like the idea of a dog's teeth sinking into my flesh so I kept my composure and walked with peace.

We were walking for a few minutes before I was greeted with big metal gates with an arrow pointing to the sign saying segregation unit, the Gov opened up the gates to allow me to push my trolley through it was kind of tight but there was just enough space for me to get past. Entering the doors of the segregation unit I remember it being very quiet you could hear a pin drop a different environment from what I was normally used to even the prison air smelt different no air conditioning hardly any windows to get fresh air, I was assigned a cell on two's landing not realising that I was next door to two other people that were already there before me as the door closed I placed my bags on the bed looking around the cell acknowledging that this is my new home.

I immediately started spring cleaning the hole cell scrubbed the walls got on my hands and knees scrubbing the floor the sink the toilet the bed frame everything got sanitised even the mattress & pillows.

I must have been cleaning for hours because I remember sweating like I was in a sauna or a steam room before a knock on the wall comes from my next-door neighbour "YO" I respond; "you ok bro he replies" I reply "yea g I'm good" what's your name and where you from, I'm "billy" from Burnley brother how about yourself? Cool bro, I'm Aaron from Manchester I've just come from HINDLEY up north and I've just had my categorisation reclassified as Category-A what's your story, Billy.

We get talking throughout the night and get to know each other's lives talking and the weirdest thing is even though he was from a different world we kind of related in some way, our lives had similar experiences in many ways plus our opinions built on real-life events and the existing experiences whether that was due to being in prison or what's happened in our own lives on the outside.

Billy was educated, but it was a shame because he did suffer from mental health issues and being next door to him certain nights I could hear him chatting to himself plus due to the conversations that we had already he said himself he's had problems in the past and he's been on medication to help him control the thoughts for a while.

We didn't have electricity in our cells at the time too so being up all night chatting was sure to pass the time, so every night we'd stay up catching joke giving each other a bit of knowledge laughing sometimes it didn't even feel like you were on category-A in a high-security prison the time went quite quick.

About a week had passed when Billy and I were walking in the exercise yard it was a misty day slightly rainy and a bit cold I remember it being late November early December and that sticks in my head because I remember him saying his birthday was on the 30th December and that was coming up plus it was Christmas time so the festive season was all over the T.V, I asked him what was the reason he was categorised as an A-cat prisoner something that I'd not asked since I'd got there despite all the conversations we had throughout the week I never asked him about his case until this day.

He explained as we walked in circles doing laps after laps that he was going through a family problem with his sister's boyfriend because he kept beating his sister up but every time he intervened he never benefited from trying help, this was going on for a while maybe a year or two before he lost it at the family party.

An argument broke out between him and his sister's boyfriend both were drunk but he tried to defuse the situation because it was a family celebration and he didn't want to cause any disrespect whatsoever to his people but got punched in the face her drunken boyfriend which frustrated and got him mad that much he went home a few minutes round the corner armed himself with a kitchen knife and heading back to his sister's house, he said he walked through the doorway went behind his sister's boyfriend that was stood in the living room and stuck the knife through the top of his head. He said he ended up stabbing him 37 times all in the upper body area of his neck and torso sliced his throat and then licked the blood of the knife in a rage screaming and shouting said he lost all control blacking out saw red and went to stab a few more people but realised most was his family and friends, he absconded before the police turned up but only went home to change his clothes and stash the knife that he just used to murder his sister's boyfriend with. But with so many witnesses at the scene plus his sister told the police everything that had happened to her boyfriend, and that very same night he was arrested and booked into the local police station in Burnley.

He pleaded guilty on the grounds of not being in control of his actions but he'll take full responsibility for the killing, he was assessed by the authorities and phycologist within the local prison whilst on remand and deemed a schizophrenic that needed to be carefully monitored he was starred up and sent to Rampton secure hospital where he stayed for 8–12 months before getting transferred to the segregation unit at (HMP WOODHILL) still classified as a juvenile because he was under eighteen as well as myself.

His next-door neighbour Jonathan was in for arson similar age to me because we were all youngsters the first category-A juvenile inmates in England and that was never heard of really because that wasn't normal for juveniles prisoners, Jonathan set a house on fire after attempting to murder a man he a had a long time feud with and ended up getting apprehended a few months later due to a beer can he left at the scene allegedly he broke in through the living room window and poured a few litres of gasoline all over down downstairs, as the people woke up to see their house in flames they managed to evacuate their home but suffering from 20% burns to their bodies as well as the kids.

No wonder I sat and thought why being a Category-A prisoner was different to being a standard prisoner at (HMP HINDLEY) because I as well as everyone else was being assessed by psychologists, and they were writing reports on Abnormality like our behaviour (or dysfunctional behaviour) which is a behavioural characteristic assigned to those with conditions regarded as rare or dysfunctional.

Behaviour is considered abnormal when it is atypical or out of the ordinary, consists of undesirable behaviour, and results in impairment in the individual's functioning.

In my prison assessment reports, they said I had a personality disorder a type of mental disorder in which you have a rigid and unhealthy pattern of thinking, functioning and behaving.

I was deemed a person with a personality disorder who has trouble perceiving and relating to situations and people.

However, I wasn't taking any notice of that because I knew exactly who I was so all the psychologist can write about who they think I am or negatively write about my crime but deep down I knew I wasn't insane or crazy it was just the life I lead disturbing to others but you have to understand that all people come from different parts of the world live different lives deprived of certain things look at the obstacles the trials and tribulations understand the people but instead, I was being labelled a no-good gang banger an is capable of murder also an individual who likes to glorifies violence.

My mental state and behavioural pattern were monitored for 6 months while I was in the segregation unit until I turned eighteen years of age and was assessed again, I showed no signs of abnormalities in my behaviour and attitude towards the treatment of being a juvenile category-A prisoner.

My stay at (HMP WOODHILL) was a temporary placement while they assessed us being juveniles until I was transferred back up north to (HMP MANCHESTER) aka (STRANGE WAYS) only to attend Court for a pre-liminary hearing the case had already been transferred to the Crown after my not guilty plea weeks prior.

Another the long journey double cuffed staring out of the small box double-sided window wearing a banana outfit was on the cards again, the difference from being on normal location to category-A inmates was there was no messing around with time or loitering interaction between you and others was strictly prohibited especially when you move everything is done by the book.

After getting back from a long road trip back from (HMP MANCHESTER) aka (STRANGE WAYS) the atmosphere within the unit was different something didn't seem right the energy was off different from the norm for some reason even the air didn't smell right it smelt like a dried-up corpse the remains of something dead, as I got closer to my cell located on the twos landing the smell got worse and worse a smell that I've never smelt before it was disgusting. I asked the screw that was escorting me back to my cell what that nasty horrible odour was and where it was coming from they mentioned something to do with an inmate on the one's landing has been smearing shit all over his cell and on himself for the last few days, it is known as a dirty protest a way of making demands in prison to try and achieve getting what you want.

I had to live with that smell for a good few days before they cleaned up the cell and the guy was moved to a different location and oh my was I pleased for him to move I couldn't take it the smell was something else very potent enough to make you want to vomit yesterday's dinner it was that bad, that's when I realised that the prison system is a weird and volatile unhealthy place to be the negativity that surrounds you the tension can be cut with a knife.

After a while, maybe a few months had past and with the future of us juveniles being category-A security and our level being monitored by the board of directors of the prison service instructed by the home office, they started to fill the spaces on the landings and because there were only 8 cells on the twos it only held up to 8 juveniles.

The year 2005 down the "block" the segregation unit it was very boring apart from reading books and skimming the pages of a magazine or newspapers maybe flipping through your letters for the 100th time plus we had no electric power running through our cells at the time so we had to use power batteries bought from the canteen to power your stereo and a crocodile clip to get a decent reception without it you couldn't find any radio stations, until the near summer of 2005, when electricity was installed in all the cells for the juvenile inmates just in time for the football the champions league final against two giants.

The 2005 UEFA Champions League Final was the final match of the 2004–05 UEFA Champions League,

Europe's primary club football competition. The show-piece event was contested between Liverpool of England and Milan of Italy at the Atatürk Olympic Stadium in Istanbul, Turkey on 25 May 2005.

As soon as we had electricity installed in our cells and we were allowed to have property sent in I was straight on the phone to my people outside ordering my music and other things, the first parcel I received was a batch of cd's and tapes with all my favourite music and artists and I can say having music was the only thing that kept me from going insane music is a powerful tool for controlling your emotional state of mind and being in my situation at the time music was surly, my psychiatrist I didn't need anything else.

We rarely got the chance to get off the wing but every time we did to go places like health care or reception to pick up your property we were always escorted by the dog handler you couldn't go anywhere without him and his Alsatian watching your every step id be lying if I said I wasn't wary at times because they were a little bit to close for comfort and it wasn't comfortable to have a big dog walking behind you it does put you on edge and anyone who's been in that position will probably tell you the same truth, it differs for others but I'm just sceptical about dogs after getting bitten on the face by a Rottweiler when I was young.

My trial date was set for September but being in May going into June I could feel the warm days fast approaching the days gradually getting longer the cells warming up it wasn't pleasant to be stuck in a box 23 hours a day all sticky sweating felt like you were a piece of meat getting cooked slowly in an oven on a low heat especially having no access to fans or any form of air conditioning, the windows only opened up to a certain point lack of oxygen made it hard to sleep tossing and turning mostly throughout the summer.

There were only three juveniles at the time on the landing until five more new juveniles arrived from London Brixton on remand for a murder they tried to rob a taxi driver but unfortunately, the man died from a variety of gunshot wounds paramedics was called to the scene but was unable to save the man's life.

I didn't have one bit of trouble with inmates while I was at HMP WOODHILL apart from one supremacist that was living on the ones landing chanting racist remarks out his door and through his window when we were doing laps on the exercise yard, these constant racist slurs were going for quite some time every day without fail he'd be at the door or window chatting shit and I think it was because he wasn't able to see us face to face or be around us at any time so that's where his bravery was coming from I suppose.

It was just another summers day morning waking up to the sight bars on the windows and the smell of the Saturday brunch hit your nostril senses plus reflects from the bright sunlight shining off the bars and metal frameworks of the cell the sound of keys rattling from the screws walking up and down dogs in the far distance barking loudly and I wasn't a morning person at all especially when and if I've not any sleep the night before plus being in prison you learn to adapt to the routine because everything is run by time order and disciplined movement, I think it was just before lunch and we was let out on the yard for our hour daily exercise it was only Billy and me out that day, the rest of the inmates was indoors because I think it may have been raining heavily that late morn I remember was we soaked and had been out for about 35 minutes or until we wanted to go back in. I had a flask with me that morning that I left inside for when I came back in as we walked in the door waiting for the screw to let us through the gate the shower room was located on the left-hand side as you walked onto the wing and I never thought today was going to be my lucky day, as I stepped onto the wing the screws was going to make a mistake by letting the supremacist out the shower straight away with no hesitation my flask collided with his wrinkled forehead the force of the strike made a cracking sound like it cracked his forehead it was a clean strike splitting his forehead straight down the middle just above his nose bridge he fell back his legs gave way and just as I was about finish with a kick or a few punches the screws jumped on me twisted and bent me up and restrained me putting me in all sorts of controlled arm locks and if you try to resist by fighting they just strap your legs and arms up so you can't move or lash out. As a remanded prisoner I couldn't get additional time added to my sentence generally dealt with externally by the outside adjudicator "the Judge" rather than internal by the governor's office, fortunately for me it was dealt with internal and was given 21 days loss of everything but the prison mindset of being locked away so they weren't that much they could to me.

It wasn't long after that I was shipped off back-up North to face trial in the upcoming months of September.

July 2005 just after my birthday month of June I've turned eighteen years old and the dreaded long journey down the M25 back to Manchester was on the cards plus wearing that smelly banana suit was not comfortable to wear whatsoever as well as wearing those metal wrist bracelets that was restricting my movement I was transferred from HMP WOODHILL to HMP MANCHESTER AKA strange ways holds category-A inmates and double A-Cat high profile, prisoners.

HMP MANCHESTER AKA.
STRANGE WAYS.

HM Prison Manchester is a high-security men's prison in Manchester, England, operated by her majesty prison service.

It is still commonly referred to as Strangeways, which was its former official name derived from the area in which it is located until it was rebuilt following a major riot in 1990. It is a local prison, holding prisoners remanded into custody from courts in the Manchester area and Category A prisoners (those whose escape would be highly dangerous).

Strangeways was designed by Alfred Waterhouse and opened in 1868 alongside the demolished Manchester Assize courts. The prison is known for its prominent ventilation tower and imposing design, structured by the principles of the separate system.

The Manchester Assize Courts was a building housing law courts on Great Ducie Street in the Strangeways district of Manchester England. It was 279 ft (85 m) tall and from 1864/1877 the tallest building in Manchester. Widely admired, it has been referred to as one of Britain's 'lost buildings'.

Just like the lost buildings and many lost rivers and streets within the city of Manchester, that's exactly how I felt at the time of starting what was going to be a long journey through the prison system. HMP Manchester wasn't so bad when I landed there considering it was only the best part of 15 years since they had one of the most expensive riots in the history of English prisons, before I landed on the main location I was held in the health care department for 3 days while they monitored me because I was only eighteen years old that was the process otherwise I would have been straight on the wing soon as I landed but there was a procedure in place everything had to be done by the book, you couldn't take a piss without them watching you or writing down in there little yellow book everything that you have done what time this what time that it was tiring and draining every day.

Being in the health care department was an experience in its self loads of crazy guys wondering about heads down staring in to fin air looking real spaced out moving like zombies, it was the first time I can say I was a bit wary because you didn't know if any of these loony bins have the thought of causing you to harm so yeah the first thing I had to do is make a shank a homemade blade that I used to stick to one of my inner thighs so it was hidden but accessible when needed.

I eventually landed on the Cat-A unit where I met and booked up into many homies from the block also my co-defendant was already on the wing waiting for me because he was told by one of the screws that I'd landed and was waiting to come to the unit, I was greeted by many homies that were remanded for various crimes but a few were there just for being associated with criminal minds and being part of an (O.C.G) organised crime gang. Many people that I didn't know was on there for various reasons, murder, extremism, money laundering, Robbers, kidnapping, shootings, drug kingpins, IRA crime lords you name it there were all walks of life surrounding you not a day didn't go by that you didn't prepare for the negative atmosphere to erupt but overall it wasn't that bad it was very calm considering.

E-wing was split into two different wings the segregation unit was below whereas one side is for the low end of society's spectrum the child killers rapist and other abnormal humans, and the other side where I was held was for the robbers, kidnappers, murderers, drug kingpins, hitmen, IRA prisoners, other political prisoners such as extremists, whatever crime you could imagine I'm sure it was here in HMP Manchester because you had all people from different countries and walks of life behind those doors. The one thing that I hated was the fact that every time you wanted something from health care you had to be on the ones landing directly facing all the child killers and rapist the nurse would be stood behind the door posting your medication through the square hatch build in the door, you would see them lining up waiting to get seen to by the nurse and I can't lie I used to get the chills because they just looked different and because I was aware of who they were my blood use to boil every time I saw them it got to the stage where I ended up not going to the hatch because I couldn't stand the sight of them stood there literally 8-10 feet away.

As category A prisoners; there are certain require-
ments that the prison service offers different to the
others on normal locations 1, being allowed to have
access to hot beverages being able to make your food
with the use of the kitchen etc, but the officers on the
unit were abusing their power and not letting us use the
kitchen which got took over by the screws so we weren't
happy with what was happening not only that peoples
credit on the pin phones wasn't being credited canteens
was being misplaced applications were getting ripped
up and ignored peoples property damaged the screws
were taking the piss really until one day we all thought
fuck this shit we have to make a stand let our voices
be heard because we are getting treated unfairly and it
was becoming a joke, some say we're in prison and we're
supposed to be some of the most violent and hardest of
criminals so why complain but when your personal life
is being tampered with especially being in that position
people get emotional.

Riot squad drama at Strangeways

I had only landed in Strangeways weeks before the peaceful protest and a RIOT squad of a crack elite, prison officers were sent into Strangeways to stop a protest by some
of its most dangerous inmates.

A team of about 80 jailers with dogs and batons were rushed to the building to deal with the demonstration.

Strangeways bosses feared for the safety of six prison officers who were with the inmates. Armed Police were drafted in to form a cordon around the prison walls.

More than 20+ inmates who were involved were later transferred to other prisons other's stayed.

We were are all category A inmates - those regarded as the most serious security risk.

Details of the drama only emerged after (kB junior) an inmate wrote to a relative and revealed how the trouble flared.

Prison authorities and the police did not release any information about the protest which happened on the Sunday 28th of August 2005 until approached by a reporter.

In the letter, the inmate wrote: "It has been kicking off in here over the weekend.

The Cat A wing had a riot, 20+ of them have been shipped out.

They are sick of the way they are being treated. They sent the dogs in and a full riot squad with smoke bombs was deployed." The demonstration began when more than 30 category A prisoners refused to go back to cells on E wing. KB isn't wrong whatsoever I was on the wing when around 20 to 25 prison guards suited and booted started swinging bats and letting the dogs off the lead on the landing, everyone ran into different cells panicking scared of getting bit by the dogs. The cell I was in was attacked last by the guards but in the background, I could hear loud bangs and dogs barking loud voices shouting coming from both inmates and the screws, by the time they got round to us they had most of the situation under control so we all came out peacefully and was escorted to our cells. The next morning on a Monday the atmosphere on the wing was like no other you hear a pin drop it the doors were closed we were on lockdown for the morning and afternoon and only let out to get our dinner's and then back to our cells, the reason why it so quiet was because half the wing already got an emergency security ship out to other categorised A establishments.

THE AFTERMATH.

A spokesman for the Prison Service said smoke bombs were not used and no one was injured. 'WHICH WAS LIE'

She added an investigation into the protest has been launched by governor Chris Sheffield.

She said: "The incident remained calm but national resources were deployed to deal with it." 'WHICH WAS CORRECT'

She further added a police spokesman said: "At approximately 2:26 pm on the Sunday of 28th August 2005, police were informed that a peaceful protest was taking place at HMP Manchester due to the condition and treatment they were receiving.

Several pre-planned procedures were put into place and armed forces officers attended the prison but remained outside the perimeter.

"There was no breach of security and the demonstration was resolved peacefully by prison staff." because we intended to have a peaceful protest without the need for any forceful violence.

Juliet Lyon, director of the Prison Reform Trust, said: "It is always regrettable when a prison feels that it has to resort to force against people for whom it is responsible, particularly as at Manchester when it appears to have been dealing with a peaceful protest." in my opinion on that day, it was the officers who turned it negatively by attacking two inmates (Rob) & (Tony) who went to speak with the officers but got threatened with batons and was made to make a break for it because they let the dogs off the lead onto the wing.

I am aware of the prison suffering from a devastating 25-day riot in 1990 when inmates clambered onto the prison roof but that also was to protest about their circumstances and the treatment within the prison system, so to me, it's just baffling why they wouldn't want to change the criteria.

They certainly didn't want to go back to 1990, when The 1990 Strangeways Prison riot was a 25-day prison riot and rooftop protest at Strangeways prison in Manchester, England. The riot began on 1 April 1990 when prisoners took control of the prison chapel, and the riot quickly spread throughout most of the prison. The riot and rooftop protest ended on 25 April when the final five prisoners were removed from the rooftop, making it the longest prison riot in British penal history. One prisoner was killed during the riot, and 147 prison officers and 47 prisoners were injured. Much of the prison was damaged or destroyed with the cost of repairs coming to £55 million.

The riot sparked a series of disturbances in prisons across England, Scotland and wales, resulting in the British government announced a public inquiry into the riots headed by Lord Woolf.

The resulting Woolf Report concluded that conditions in the prison had been unendurable, and recommended major reform of the prison system.

I can say it did get a little better after time but only for a few weeks before it kind of went back to how it was previously described before the peaceful protest, my court date was fast approaching so it wasn't long before I was due to be up in front of the judge jury's prosecutions and wigs plus my defence team.

A few weeks after the incident on the wing it's like all the screws would always want to fuck with me and my co-defendant writing us up for the most ridiculously and most pathetic petty things such as not getting our dinner or loud music anything that we seemed to do would be their excuse to put us in front of the (P.O) principal officer, I think we spent most of our time on the basic regime with no television just a stereo system and having to entertain ourselves with limited resources.

After a few weeks had passed since the peaceful protest against the system, time started to slowly move it was like time halted maybe because I was a bit nervous knowing it was only a matter of weeks before I was in the courthouse fighting for my freedom of liberty.

Even though I was angry and felt very disrespected by people outside as well as feeling sold out by my so-called "homies" I was still level headed about the situation I was in, it didn't matter about the consequences of my actions for being a gang member and putting In that work for my people because my actions were built on love morals and respect nothing more nothing less and I didn't do it for the fame or recognition I done it based on providing my assistance for the protection of my loved ones.

But being in my position facing a long stretch in prison for my crime it was my mother and family that suffered extensively from the disloyalty from my so-called people who were supposed to be there for you when the shit hits the ceiling but in my case, I think the kitchen got a bit too hot for those which then resulted in them snitching on me hence why I'm in custody facing life or even football numbers.

Before my trial date which was coming up in September, the prison security moved me and my co-defendant down the block on G.O.A.D (good order and discipline) after searching my cell and finding a homemade shank because I heard our rival gang members were arriving on the unit which I got told from a little birdie, we were kept in the segregation unit where I had to do seven days (solitary confinement) separately after pleading guilty to the shank they found in our cell we were kept on (G.O.A.D) until trial.

The trial began on 12th September 2005, the trial was scheduled to last for a week waking up at six o'clock in the morning every single day Monday - Friday getting ready for the journey through the streets of Manchester to the crown court where my fate was in the hands of the public. Being young black and lost and being labelled a menace to society especially being gang-related you weren't safe In the British Courts, a black capnote is the ultimate symbol of doom for a condemned man.

Seeing a judge put it on lets all present in the courtroom know that, barring some miraculous appeal or other happenstance, the fate of the prisoner at the dock has been sealed.

I could tell my fate was sealed the first moment the prosecution opened up the case with a damaging negative impact on the life I was leading running around with firearms having little regard to human life and society, the bad character was surely a way for the prosecution to get the jury to look at me and my co-defendant like we were crazy and needed to be locked up.

I was originally sentenced to 17 years in prison for the shooting offence and firearms offences but seven years got knocked off for my early guilty plea agreement together with my age being a contributing factor, I was transferred from (HMP MANCHESTER) aka strange ways to (HMP Moorlands) in Lindholm a Yorkshire jail up north not far from Leeds and Bradford.

My security was reclassified and my co-defendant and I were taken of category A and downgraded back to the normal regime without the use of any dogs or cuffs, and worse those smelly banana jumpsuits which I hated with a passion.

I remained in (HMP Moorlands) for the best part of 3 years strong this is where I met a few lifers and many different types of relatable people who you could hold and have a good conversation with real people who were just like me in many ways so I got on well within their most of the time, there were a few niggaz from different sets that would try test me but it was simply a straight fight or I was stabbing man or smashing something over your head I wasn't going to be a victim especially being from Manchester, not everybody liked you plus there were only a few Manchester lads in (MOORLANDS) between 2005 & 2008.

I can't forget my loyalties and most definitely can't skip the opportunity to give my utmost respect to my Leeds family DOM & SATA two brothers who I booked up into whilst I was on house block three in (HMP MOORLANDS), there was a lot of people who I could relate to in moorlands due to certain peoples lives and crimes which made certain relationships flow without any awkward moments or forced conversations. The two people that I did click with was DOM & SATA on the basis we had a lot more in common with each other had more of a bond because we related to the same similar situations within our own lives plus the relationship we had was not forced or fake it was solid as a rock and he's proved that many times in many situations by putting prisoners to sleep with one bang we took our friendship very seriously.

(HMP DOVEGATE)

Dovegate Prison is a Category B men's private prison, located near Uttoxeter in Staffordshire, England. The prison is operated by Serco.

Her Majesty's Prison Dovegate opened in 2001 as a private prison, operated by the Serco Group under a 25-year Design, build and manage, PFI contract.

In 2009 with the creation of an additional accommodation block, and the expansion of other facilities, the prison increased its capacity to 860 places in the main prison, with 200 places in the Therapeutic prison.

Dovegate receives Category B convicted prisoners serving four years and over with at least 18 months left to serve. Accommodation at the prison is divided into the main prison (860 places) and the Therapeutic Prison (200 places). In 2009 the addition of a further accommodation block and other facilities, saw the original capacity increase, and the prison now has 130 remand places, taking remand prisoners from Stoke and Newcastle under Lyme courts.

The education department of the jail has space for 126 prisoners to receive part-time education in classes operating 5 days a week. Activities range from basic skills to Open University courses. Other facilities include a library, shop, gym and sports centre. Dovegate has a 24-hour primary healthcare facility, with a full-time medical officer.

Chaplaincy services include a full-time Church of England chaplain and a full-time Islamic minister, part-time Methodist and Roman Catholic ministers, as well as visiting Jewish, Buddhist, Sikh and Jehovah's witnesses ministers.

There is a dedicated place of worship with Christian and multi-faith areas.

There is a staffed visitor's centre. The main visiting area has both indoor and outdoor children's play areas. It also has a bus stop directly outside the gates with Services every 2 hours to Uttoxeter and Burton on Trent.

I was transferred from (HMP Moorlands) to (HMP DOVEGATE) in 2008 late November where I stayed for around 18 months and still had 3 years left to serve before my release, I put In an application for a transfer a few years before being moved to DOVEGATE my application was denied and told I had to reapply.

When I was told I was going to another establishment I thought I was heading to where I put in for which was (HMP FRANKLAND) but got told I was heading to (HMP DOVEGATE) near Birmingham which was not a concern of mine whatsoever, I just cracked on packed my bags and hopped on the meat wagon.

I reapplied a few months after I landed at DOVEGATE which was an 18-month long wait but the time went kind of fast to be honest because I was in a good place my mind was good I was in good health eating well-doing gym plus I knew I only had a few years left to go plus I'd already been in 5 going on six years, DOVEGATE was a good place to be for gym and other educational courses and this is where I have done most things to downgrade my security level plus work towards getting certificates that can help me upon my release from prison.

My time in DOVEGATE was spent doing gym and educational courses so the time went pretty quickly for me especially being a private ran prison the regime was completely different you got to spend more time out your cell the food was much better than where I've been in the past and that's "something" because most jails don't take pride in their food whatsoever plus you could get stuff like fresh veg from the kitchens to bring back to the wing so you could cook up a storm in your kettle, tuna curries, was the main course for everyone who cooked with the kettle but that all changed when I finally received the application back for me to hop on the next meat wagon way up north to Geordi land (HMP FRANKLAND) in the November of 2009.

(HMP FRANKLAND) (CATEGORY A DISPERSAL)

HM Prison Frankland is a category A men's prison located in the village of Brasside in County Durham, England. Frankland is operated by Her majesty's prison service. Frankland was originally opened in 1980 with four wings each holding 108 in single cells.

A further two wings opened in 1998 to an open gallery design to hold an additional 206. A specialist Dangerous and Severe Personality Disorder (DSPD) unit opened at the prison in May 2004.

The prison has increased in size in recent years following major redevelopment work including the construction of the new DSPD 'Westgate Unit'. In March 2008, the Ministry of Justice announced that Frankland would be expanded again, with planning permission being granted for an extra 120 places at the prison.

In 2011, before I left two convicted prisoners, Nathan Mann and Michael Parr, disembowelled 23-year-old Mitchell Harrison, who had been convicted of raping a 13-year-old girl.

It was headline news at the time all over the local media stretching as far as my own home of Manchester, watching the news and seeing (HMP FRANKLAND) whilst I was in there was a crazy feeling especially because I knew that majority of the prisoners were very unstable and was category A carrying life sentences with recommendations ranging from 20 to 40 years + it was a mad place everybody's prisoner I.D card on the doors said (LIFE) it wasn't a good idea to act like you was the man there the atmosphere was different people went of respect and there was a lot off respectable gentlemen who's just made a mistake which had cost them their lives.

Frankland is a dispersal prison that holds male prisoners who are over 21 years of age, and whose sentence is usually 4 years or more, life sentences and high-risk remand prisoners. Prison accommodation is divided between wings, with wings A to D holding 108 inmates each, wings F and G holding an additional 208, with J holding 120. All cells are single occupancy.

The Healthcare Centre at the prison consists of a 4-bedded ward and 10 furnished rooms, a dental suite, X-ray and a suicide Crisis Suite. Several clinics are held, many conducted by visiting specialists. There are also telehealth services and wing-based treatment rooms. Primary care is contracted to the County Durham & Darlington Foundation Trust.

Education at the prison is provided by Milton Keynes college, with a range of courses provided - from basic skills to a higher education level. Frankland also runs workshops in furniture production, a charity workshop and a sight-and-sound workshop. The prison has a library and gym to support inmates' learning and recreation also has a visitors' centre. Facilities include a canteen and children's play area, all with disabled access.

One of the best things that I found about living in Frankland was being able to cook and organise your food instead of eating the same usual jail slop, the canteen provided you with all of your favourite and special ingredients for you to cook up some of the best dishes you missed or would like to eat if you were at home. Chicken, lamb, beef, veg, rice, fruit, drinks, fish, all the healthy stuff what was good for you especially when you're in the gym because you can only eat so much prison food it isn't good for your guts too much oil in there for food they seem to deep fat fry most things or boil the natural goodness out the food there's no nutrition, and all you do is end up shitting it out straight away that's why most inmates live of the famous recipe of tuna and noodles or kettle-cooked curries.

Getting sent to Frankland was a great experience for me because I got to see both sides of the prison system in their differences and the unique categories to the way they operate behind and within those walls, despite what I have seen due to the violence in that volatile place where many men are going through different types of problems sentences deemed to be inhumane but all the in all, I've taken one of the biggest educational lessons from being in Frankland and I'm honoured to have met some of the country's most dangerous criminals that have ever lived in the prison system.

Whether you're perceptions as a reader may differ from those as well as mines, it's in my opinion that those that are deemed to be the dangers of society are paying for crimes that they've committed or may not have committed and I'm not referring to or talking about the child molesters and sex offenders I'm talking about those honourable loyal inmates who have just simply made a mistake whether that's protecting their family & friends or simply trying to make a better life for themselves and kids, because you never know or should judge another person's life as I say in my motto "you should never knock another man's hustle, because you never know another man's struggle" a lot of people my not of had the right start in life so wanting more for yourself or your family should not be looked down on but as you know you can't continuously retain and maintain a good life through all that illegal activity because it leads to one place and one place only to the concrete grave know as (PRISON).

(HMP LIVERPOOL)
(Living with the wildlife)

HM Prison Liverpool (formerly Walton Gaol) is a category B/C local men's prison in Walton, Liverpool England. It is operated by Her Majesty's prison service.

Liverpool Prison (originally known as Walton Gaol) was constructed between 1848 and 1855 to the designs of John Weightman borough surveyor (not to be confused with his near-contemporary John Grey Weightman) to replace an 18th-century establishment in the centre of Liverpool, which had become too small for current needs. It originally housed male and female inmates.

On 4 February 1939, the IRA attempted but failed, to break a wall of the prison during the S - plan bombing campaign in Britain that year.

During the Liverpool Blitz of World War II, on 18 September 1940, German high explosive bombs falling on a wing of the prison partially demolished it, killing

22 inmates. The body of one was not found until 11 years later when the rubble was finally cleared.

The prison was the site of 62 judicial executions, from 1887 to 1964. The last execution at the prison was that of Peter Anthony Allen. He and his accomplice Gwynn Owen Evans were convicted for the murder of Jhon Allan West in April 1964. They were simultaneously hanged on 13 August 1964; Allen was hanged at Walton Gaol and Evans at Strangeways in Manchester.

Liverpool Prison was overcrowded and had poor industrial relations which had led to an unacceptable regime. The inspection found that parts of the jail were generally unclean, had a cockroach & rat infestation and broken windows which can be confirmed by me and many others that have been to HMP Liverpool.

Inmates were able to shower and change their clothes just once a week at the prison.

After doing further research I found that an inspection report in February 2010, stated that drugs, bullying and violence were still prevalent at Liverpool Prison, despite the jail improving in other areas. Days later, it emerged that the Prison Service had refunded nearly £10,000 to inmates at HMP Liverpool, who were being overcharged for watching television in their cells.

The prison was charging £1 per prisoner per week instead of per cell, meaning that inmates who were sharing a cell were paying more than they needed to.

Liverpool, well, I have to say it was one of the worst jails if not (THE) worse ever that I have been to in my life and I plan never to return to that infested establishment it's like living with wildlife "literally" instead of inmates it is a crazy place.

TIME IS PRECIOUS.

It's complicated, and there are multiple causes of major depression.

Factors such as genetic vulnerability, severe life stressors, substances you may take (some medications, drugs and alcohol) and medical conditions can affect the way your brain regulates your moods.

There's no single cause of depression.

It can occur for a variety of reasons and it has many different triggers.

For some people, an upsetting or stressful life event, such as bereavement, divorce, illness, redundancy and job or money worries, can be the cause.

Different causes can often combine to trigger depression. Well, it's difficult for me to explain how my mother was feeling at the time of myself going to prison a long time at a young age I can't possibly even begin to imagine how she felt but I can give you an insight into the world of my experiences with the feeling of not seeing my mothers face for nearly 8 long year's it was upsetting and very stressful and I'm sure being a mother it was much harder for herself to go through the journey without seeing my face either just the thought is depressing alone never mind having to live through it every day.

The reason I include this paragraph in my prison chapter is that I would like to give you as the reader a look at the effects of the years I spent away locked up like an animal without seeing my mothers face for almost 8 year's, only phone calls hearing each other's voices kept me alive and continuing to strive nothing else I could have done, me not seeing my mum for nearly 8 year's had nothing to do with her not wanting to visit me it was more to the fact that she fell into a depressive state of mind and couldn't face me being locked away especially for so many years which was understandable because her baby just got 10 year's custody and don't forget it was my people who made it easier for the jury to convict me and for the judge to slam the gavel down.

My point is that 'time is precious, meaning simply, that time it's valuable.

It can also mean a certain period (for instance time with a loved one) is especially valuable. It can also refer to the need not to waste time.

Time is the most precious resource because you can't get it back. ... The answer to this question matters because you can't get wasted time back. People often think of money as their most valuable resource, and while it is important because it allows you to buy the things you need and want, you can get money-back guaranteed but not your time. Time is a very precious thing in our life. Time is something we should never waste in any way. We can spend a lot of time doing various works, but we can never get back the time we spent.

That's why most successful people consider time as more important and valuable than money. Most people who respect and value time can learn faster and work faster. They become more focused and pay more attention to their work. ... You develop a better understanding of how things are the way they are and why they happen because you spend quality time doing things. "Time is more precious than gold, more precious than diamonds, more precious than oil or any valuable treasures. It is time that we do not have enough of; it is time that causes the war within our hearts, and so we must spend it wisely."

Don't waste your time and most importantly, it's not worth wasting your precious time in prison when you could be out in the world creating remembrances living life not caged up with a one-hour visitation and twenty-pound canteen to spend every week that's two hundred pounds a year do the mathematical studies weigh up your options think about how you want to be spending your time, life is short on this earth.

Always remember that everybody has the same 24 hours but it's how you use that makes the difference because, in my opinion, it separates the ones that want more in life from the one's that are stuck in the same position continuing to make excuses making the same mistakes.

After not seeing my mums face for almost 8 year's from being in custody when I was finally released I was under (M.A.P.P.A)

WHAT IS MAPPA?

Multi-Agency Public Protection Arrangements, or MAPPA, are a set of arrangements to manage the risk posed by the most serious sexual and violent offenders under the provisions of sections 325 to 327B of the Criminal Justice Act 2003.

They bring together Police, Probation, and Prison Services in each of the 42 areas in England and Wales into what is called the MAPPA Responsible Authority.

Several other agencies must cooperate with this authority including social services, health trusts, youth offending teams, Jobcentre Plus, local housing and education authorities.

Two Lay Advisers are appointed by the Responsible Authority to sit on each MAPPA area Strategic Management Board (SMB) alongside senior representatives from agencies. They are members of the public who act as independent, informed observers able to pose questions. professionals. They bring to the SMB their understanding and perspective of the local community.

HOW MAPPA WORKS.

MAPPA-eligible offenders are identified and information about them shared by the agencies to inform risk-assessment and risk-management plans of those managing or supervising them.

In the majority of cases that is as far as MAPPA extends, but in some, it is determined that active multi-agency management is required. In those cases, there will be regular MAPPA meetings attended by relevant agency practitioners.

There are three categories of MAPPA-eligible offender:

Category 1 – registered sex offenders

Category 2 – mainly violent offenders sentenced to imprisonment for 12 months or more

Category 3 – offenders who do not qualify under categories one or two, but who pose a risk of serious harm.

There are three management levels to ensure resources are focused on the cases where they are needed most, generally those involving the higher risks of serious harm.

Level 1 – involves ordinary agency management ie. no MAPPA meetings or resources

Level 2 – where the active involvement of more than one agency is required to manage the offender but the risk management plans do not require the attendance and commitment of resources at a senior level

Level 3 – where senior oversight is required

MAPPA is also supported by (ViSOR) which is a national IT system to help manage people who pose a serious risk of harm to the public. The Police have been using ViSOR since 2005, but from 2008 key staff from Police, Probation, and Prison Services can use the same IT system, which improves the quality and timeliness of risk. Assessments and interventions to prevent offending.

It increases the ability to share intelligence across organisations and enable the safe transfer of key information when high-risk offenders move.

Being under close supervision by the police and other authorities, upon my release I had to live in a hostel for three months plus they knew through my recorded prison history that I hadn't seen my mum for years so I argued the fact that I have to see my mum the day I'm released back into the community, my wish was granted on the basis that I have to get escorted by (Xcalibre) the Manchester gang police to my mum's address and they would wait outside for one hour while I saw my family. The day I got out I was so nervous about seeing my mum it had been years since I'd saw her my heart was pounding my hairs were standing up on the back of my neck I had goosebumps all over my body, I reached home and was greeted by my family & friends but the most warming feeling I got was hugging my mum I held her for about two-three minutes as water began to fill up in my eyes which suddenly just begun to flood down on to my cheeks I couldn't hold the emotion within me it was a sad moment but also one of the most beautifully blessed moments in my life.

That's why I say TIME IS PRECIOUS, it's the most important thing in your life don't waste it.

Before I bring this chapter to a close I would like to give my opinion on what I practised and what helped me get through the system, which I think may help those that are in the prison system today or for anybody that finds themselves on their way to the big house for whatever reason even down to those who know people in prison and would like to show some love and support in a positive light because I can say it goes along with.

These are a few lessons that I have learned along the way from prison that I would like to share with you because I do believe that they have changed my perception of life and what it means to be prosperous and to make it home in one piece.

- Let go of control. It's impossible to control things from prison. ...
- There are consequences for every action. ...

- Self-acceptance and confidence. ...
- Vulnerable and emotionally open. ...
- Make the best out of every situation.
- Stay humble.
- "Every moment is a fresh beginning." ...
- "Nothing is impossible, the word itself says 'I'm possible!'" ...
- "You can't use up creativity. ...
- "In the middle of a difficulty lies opportunity."

To all my close family and friends, doing life behind the gates of hell & being suffocated by those walls of doom and to many more knocking down those years across the globe keep continuing to strive to achieve on being released from those chains & cuffs, because I'm positive one day that you'll be free and be reunited with your loved ones the struggle continues so don't give up keep fighting for your (LIBERTY)... (beautiful birds ain't meant to be caged)...

Singed- Aaron Nathan Grossman...
Aka- Locz Da 6th...

Aaron whilst at
HMP Dovegate,
2008

Aaron visited by Natalie and
Tyhea at Dovegate, 2009

Aaron, HMP
Moorlands, 2007

CHAPTER NINE

The Story Continues.
The Path of Acceptance,
Keeping The Faith & Positivity.

Positivity means thinking optimistically, looking for solutions, expecting good results and success, and focusing and making life happier. It is a happy and worry-free state of mind, which looks at the bright side of life.

How do we express positivity, Focus on the good things? Challenging situations and obstacles are a part of life. ...

LAZERS & BEAMZ

In September 2012 I was awakened by my soon-to-be son's mother Esha, I'd only been out of prison for 8 months so the thought of any suspicious activity or being targeted by anyone was not in my mind as I wipe the sleep from the corner of my eye.

I thought I was having a Lucid dream but this shit was real life, lucid dreams are when you know that you're dreaming while you're asleep. You're aware that the events flashing through your brain aren't happening. But the dream feels vivid and real. As I jump off my bed getting up to check out the surroundings of my apartment, Esha grabs me again on my right thigh but this time with more of a clenched squeeze like she's scared of a scene from watching a Stephen Spielberg horror movie.

All the lights were off in my apartment apart from the dim light on the clock which was showing 5.05 am, I remembered going to bed around 3.30 am that morning as I was up most of the night studying the driving theory test on the laptop computer which I had coming up in a few weeks after failing the first time by 3 points. The silence of my apartment made my thought process even more sceptical about someone being in my flat because you could hear a pin drop it was that quiet and peaceful, as I approached the bedroom door to open it inwards towards me my eyes latched on to 6 red light infrared dots beaming and shining on against the door. The minute I saw the infrared dots shining brightly against the door I didn't even have any time to react to the loud shouting and screaming of the police right outside the front door, Esha didn't know what to do with herself panicked and ran straight diagonally into the bathroom surprisingly she made it without getting mistakenly identified as a suspect. As Esha ran into the bathroom, I panic trying to scoop up all the weed that I had out on the side from the night before which was about 20 grams of Amnesia Haze at that moment, I could feel my blood pumping from my heart together with a racing pounding heartbeat very much felt like it was going to just pump out my chest cavity.

As all the shouting continued from the armed response unit it startled me to the point where I lost concentration of what I was doing for a slight second until I realised that they were hesitant to come into the flat properly, which gave me a bit more time because they were just shouting (armed police) (armed police) (come out) (NOW) continuously which made Esha panic more and she ran out towards them into the hallway as she got seen running in and out of the bathroom I'm amazed that they didn't suspect her of holding anything but on the other hand we wasn't posing any threat towards anyone but it was pitch black so it made it scarier. While Esha was getting secured by the arms officers out on the front I was still Panicking scooping up the last of the bud and other Little bits which I could have gone back to jail for because at this time I still had another 10 months left on my probation, miraculously they didn't even find the bud which I stashed in the rack of clothes in the wardrobe in the same smell proof zip sealed bag what I received it in. After getting screamed at multiple times by the (A.R.O) armed response officers

I was dragged outside in my boxers half naked with no socks or slippers on being placed in the damp grassy area at the entrance of my flat and I think we were just coming out of the summer months so September wasn't too bad but at 5 a.m. it wasn't pleasant to be cuffed in the muddy grassy area of my apartment, they ran our names through the system de-arrested me and put us back inside my flat after they secured the premises.

The most interesting thing about this story is that when the (A.R.O) armed response officers secured the premises together with me and my soon to be sons mother Esha, they said they were here after receiving intel that I was back on the gang activities and that I've been seen with a firearm and dealing with drugs plus there was no sign of any plainclothes officers there were no dogs present nor were they any female officers so they couldn't even search Eash. They searched for drugs and went through my belongings, searching for other stuff that they thought was going to be incriminating for a chance to lock me up but all they took was my laptop, phones, and a few other electronic devices. Fortunately, the weed was in a smell proof bag tucked in deep into Esha's clothes in the wardrobe and because they were no dogs present I believe that's the reason why they didn't find it, I was lucky I suppose. But honestly, I do think that they came to kill me and I think if Esha wasn't there with me I think it would have been a different scenario. I do.

Since being released from prison in 2012 I was trying my very best to overcome the changes which hit me like a ton of bricks my world had changed from what I knew it to be.

May 2013 I was out no longer than 15 months before getting arrested again I found myself caught up in a drug operation where I was set up and ended up serving class A drugs to an undercover police officer opposing to be a crack head dope fiend. It was my mistake and I take full responsibility for the lack of patience, I used to think fast money and that's what was my downfall because I was broke I needed money plus I had a baby on the way at the time everything in my existence amounted to a few pounds I was literally at a dead-end still on probation once a week living off benefits the struggle was real life but when then I got arrested for the supply of class A drugs my whole world fell apart.

I left my soon to be baby's mother alone 2 months away from the beginning of a new life entering the family tree, I was locked up again I couldn't believe it the feeling was unbearable my mind state was very unbalanced I didn't know what to do with myself I didn't even eat the prison food for about 2-4 weeks my stomach, wow let's just say it wasn't pleasant at all I could not keep anything down my body was refusing to consume that prison slop I had to live off porridge oats noodles and tuna.

I was sentenced to 40 months in prison for the offence and to make matters worse, 6 months before I got arrested for the supply of class A drugs I was in a car accident where I ended up breaking my back snapping my vertebrae together with my lumber three which is still broke till this present day due to taking a 2-3minute pursuit by the police in my home town of Old Trafford, a car containing a family pulled out of the side street and smashed into me causing me to hit an oak tree head-on the family of four suffered minor injuries whereas I had to get cut out of the car by the firemen and due to me having no insurance or having a driving license at the time of the accident I was issued a summons to go court but couldn't attend due to being on my bed at home recovering from my back injuries.

When I eventually got stronger and found the energy to move around still very fragile I found it hard to walk properly my legs kept giving way at times causing me to lose balance but they still sent me to prison. At that moment, it's like I had a sudden change of thought spoke to myself, and asked myself a few simple questions " what is it that I want from life" "and where am I heading to" those two years in custody had a big impact on the way my thought process was and it was also those two years which made me think about the time I've already lost being caged up like an animal plus I had a new life outside waiting for me a beautiful, baby boy.

After my release in 2015, and eventually making it out of the hostel I focused my energy on;

1. Practising gratitude...
2. Keeping a gratitude journal.
3. Opening myself up to humour...
4. Spending more time with positive people...
5. Practising positive self-talk...
6. Identify my areas of negativity...
7. Starting every day on a positive note.
8. Occasionally, reading books and going to the gym releasing any negative thoughts and bad energies.

It was difficult for me at this stage of my development and growth because I just got out of prison to the sad news of my childhood, a very good friend of mine being murdered shot dead by his so-called friends.

That broke my heart and all I wanted to do is go crazy kill everything and on the flip side too that, it was that thought that made me think deeper into my own life and the way the game is, and how your people can turn on you in a blink of an eye and your not to know, that was a turning point in my life because I believe in energy and those that harm their own will succumb to their miserable demise and it won't be a good death.

So ever since that day I made a vow to myself, that I would practice the positive instead of thinking on the worse all the time because negativity affects your healthy mind and body and I was sick of feeling like my life weren't worth anything other than what's on paper for other people to judge me for it was time to make a difference give back in some way and after everything I've been through and still going through I feel it's my prerogative to give some knowledge to the people of the world as well as give advice to the youth that there is a better life ahead of you all you have to do is believe in yourself, and have a little faith you can make a difference it's in you it just needs pulling out start separating your wants from your needs.

They say a positive attitude will lead to success because people will be more willing to work with positive people rather than negative people, more effort will be put into the work of a positive person rather than a negative one and positive attitudes will lead to more motivation to complete more tasks. Also, the psychological benefits – Positive people have more energy and are more self-confident and hopeful. Because of this, they tend to set higher goals and expend more effort to reach their goals. This helps positive people see multiple solutions to problems and make better decisions. For example, positive attitudes can include:

- It is looking adversity in the eye.
- laughing.
- Getting what you get, and not pitching a fit.

- Enjoying the unexpected, even when it's not what you wanted originally.
- Motivating those around you with a positive word.
- Challenging your energy.

When you channel your energy into a positive mind frame "Positive things happen because you take charge of your thinking, also you take control of your thoughts you make good things happen. ... You become a powerful positive force. The power of positive thinking is remarkable. The idea that your mind can change your world almost seems too good to be true. ... Healthy, happy people think about what they want, and how to get it, most of the time. In this way developing a positive attitude can truly change your entire life.

Positive communication is the ability to convey messages, even negative ones, positively. ... Positive communication has the power to convert even negative feelings into positive ones and helps you create a positive impression for yourself. So you yourselves should practice well I try to develop the habit of communicating positively.

Constructive thinking, or an optimistic attitude, is the practice of focusing on the good in any given situation. It can have a big impact on your physical and mental health. ... It simply means you approach the good and the bad in life with the expectation that things will go well.

I've also learned after doing some research that your health can improve its immune system given your body greater resistance to the common cold.

Better psychological and physical well-being.

Better cardiovascular health and reduced risk of death from cardiovascular disease Better coping skills during hardships and times of stress.

These studies are all facts and I know from being in certain circumstances we can find ourselves in a state of depression because life's problems can have a big impact on the mindset especially if you're trying to change for the better we all deserve a better existence but like they say if you want something you have to go get it because nobody ain't gonna hand it to you on a plate.

Positive thinking does not necessarily mean avoiding or ignoring the bad things; instead, it involves making the most of the potentially bad situations, trying to see the best in other people, and viewing yourself and your abilities in a positive light.

That's what I've been practising more than anything because we have to deal with people every day some worse than others, but it's down to you as the individual to overcome peoples attitudes or if someone is having a bad day don't necessarily mean that you're the problem because you never know what others are dealing with within their lives.

The problem with positive thinking as an approach is that it operates at the surface level of conscious thoughts.

It does nothing to contend with the subconscious mind where negative self-talk and limiting beliefs live. If you've tried thinking positively, you know that it can be a difficult habit to maintain it's easier said than done. Putting it all together... Believe it or not, there is such a thing as too much positivity. When we lean too heavily on positive thinking alone, it can lead to a certain avoidance tendency in our lives, and lead too to self-victimization and internalization of baggage that is not yours to carry. We've all been there before when helping a friend seems like it's becoming your problem, and you feel that you're taking on most of the negative side effects of their lives we got to find the balance but on the other hand, the friend should know and be a bit more appreciative that you're taking time out to listen and perhaps give them some assistance or guidance it can be a touchy subject.

Since coming out of prison in 2015, and overcoming certain obstacles that could have had me sitting back in the slammer again for not thinking or me acting out on impulsiveness, I'm proud to say that putting those positive thoughts into action not only just saying I'll do it but putting it into action I can honestly say that it's working for me in ways that I'm in control of my emotions "well" I'm still practising and learning at the same time, but

I can feel the difference in my moods plus I'm in a better place than I once was a few years ago.

Despite all the bad things that have happened over the last five years it's a sign that there is sunshine after the rain, I've been stabbed seven times in the last 5 years since my release in the arms neck face & chest and that's on two different occasions the first incident was when I went to visit a friend who's just had a new baby boy up in the (Tong Moor) area of Bolton up north not too far from Horwich and the stadium of the Bolton Wanderers.

I was attacked by 4 white males carrying machetes knives and swords as I sat in my vehicle just came out of the shop after getting a cold drink as I was thirsty from the 30-minute drive from Manchester, I was sitting in my car scrolling through my phone smoking half of a cigarette when I was approached by 4 white males and what's crazy about this story is that they didn't even say anything to me just straight started smashing the car window stabbing me through the broken windows and the only reason I probably survived was due to one of the attackers getting his axe stuck in my windscreen and the civilians hearing the loud glass smashing noises on the street and coming out of their homes to investigate, I nearly lost my left arm also my tongue after getting stabbed in the mouth plus I got scraped with the blade in the chest area.

I was lucky enough to have survived the ordeal, some-one or something was watching over me that night because that was an unprovoked attack on me by those white guys which makes me believe that this was a racist attack and an attempt to cause me serious injuries for reasons only they would have the answers to but I can say it wasn't pleasant and it wasn't a good place to be in and it did kind of affect my day to day routine and my positive attitude towards life I wanted revenge but that also made me think and be thankful for my life it's a blessing to be hereafter that life-threatening ordeal.

I was in a bad way blood was pouring out of my mouth that much I was nearly choking & swallowing my blood at the same time trying to spit the blood out but my jaw muscles were weak plus my left arm was numb and I could only use my right arm plus I had to drive to the hospital which was like 15 minutes away because I didn't want to leave my car my mind was racing I didn't know what to do with myself it was all a mess I thought my life was over I didn't want to die without telling anyone and because my injuries were so bad I made a call to Kali one of my best friends and this is what she said after I told her I've just been stabbed and don't forget I'm in an extremely bad way and I honestly didn't think I was going to make it so I wanted to tell someone what had happened to me and for her to tell my family and friends just in case it was my last days of existence on this earth.

"At approximately 8 o'clock on the 31st of October, I was in a spa hotel in Cheshire on a weekend getaway with my boyfriend when the phone started ringing.

I looked at the phone and seen it was Aaron, I'm always excited to speak to him when he calls because our conversations range from hilariously funny stuff to really meaningful and deep talks.

He's one of my best friends he's like family to me so I answered the phone and said "hey" and straight away his first 3 words that I heard were "I've been stabbed" the blood drained out my face and my PTSD kicked in my mind started racing and I had a thousand questions I needed to ask, but all that came out was tears from my eyes and "where are you right now" "get to the nearest hospital" "what the hells happened" I'd never felt so helpless because he sounded like he was in so much pain & and was bleeding heavily so I was trying to give him the best advice and I felt like I needed to be there in person.

He said he was driving and was feeling dizzy and lightheaded that's when I got scared and all I could think is (O.M.G) is he going to die from loss of blood? I was messaging his family, and friends frantically in a state of panic as I was on the phone with him not knowing what was going to happen.

Aaron told me who to call and said call him back. As soon as he put the phone down I just burst into tears my boyfriend was hugging me confused about what's happened until I told him about my phone call I pulled myself together and made the calls but no one was answering I was in such a panic I just phoned Aaron back reassuring him he's going to be ok and asking how far from the hospital was he? trying to keep him on the phone until he arrives at the hospital & plus I felt so angry that this has happened to Aaron of all people and then I felt so low and sad that I couldn't be there in person to physically help him, hug him and tell him face to face how much me and my kid's love him and need him to be strong.

I knew this stabbing was more than physical I knew it would have a domino effect on his mental state after seeing the positive vibes he now has, & how disheartening it could be for something so cruel in life to happen to him.

The world is a mad place and I feel like the good die young but I knew it wasn't his day and thank god he was ok".

Signed Kyleshia knight-Greig...

The first incident was someone I knew as a friend well I'd like to say it's just someone I had a relationship with from being in the same area and probably from knowing the same people who operate within the city, the relationship turned sour for reasons being that people love to converse with others about you but won't come to your face and talk through a situation but would rather spend time listening to gossip from haters in the streets.

Sunday 6th of March 2016 about half seven in the evening I was picking a weed up of my mate P when this person approached my driver's side window with his hands in his pants talking with an attitude towards me threatening me telling me to get out of the car and that he wanted to speak with me about something I've to suppose to have said or done, he noticed that I had my girl in the car at the time as well but continued to press the situation causing her distress.

I told him I'm not getting out of the car and anything that you want to tell me you can ask here, which at this point all I was getting was fuck you fuck this, and fuck that there was no reasoning behind the conversation he was too irate as well as being ignorant.

I repeatedly asked him to lower his voice and aggressive tone because I've got my girl with me and she's getting kind of nervous so show some respect otherwise, this conversation is dead, and without hesitation, he stabs my car tyres at the rear with a knife that I didn't see because he had it concealed in his jacket pocket and then tells me to drive off shouting and continuously being aggressive.

I knew at this point I wasn't in a good position to be in not only that I could feel my anger and frustration building but I was blocked in by 2 big vans so I couldn't just drive off I had to manoeuvre the car plus my tyres were now popped which was making it more difficult for me manoeuvre and get out of the way of harm's way, but also my girl is a bit frightened at this point because of his erratic behaviour so that was another concern of mine and I just wanted to get her to safety.

As I positioned the car to drive through the gap between the two vans he leans in through the driver's side window and stabs me twice which felt like a punch straight through the cheek on the right side missing my jugular by inches the seatbelt made me jerk as the car stalled and being a push-button engine your foot has to be on the clutch for the car to read your keys as it had an immobilizer.

As I'm trying to start the car back up he pursues to try and stab me continuously through the window as I put my arms up in front of my face in defence to protect myself leaving my neck wide open for him to poke me straight in it, I felt a sharp pain in my neck as the blood suddenly started to spray all over the place it's like he realised what he'd just done and disappeared from the scene on his bike like a ghost.

I immediately thought that's it he's killed me Roo, my girl I was with panicking in the passenger seat holding pressure on the wounds plus the car was uncontrollable because my back rear tyres were punctured I was losing control driving like a maniac trying to make it to St Mary's hospital in a desperate attempt to survive because I knew I had to get medical assistance as soon as possible.

Luckily, I made it to the hospital and pulled through and recovered from that unnecessary attempt on my life.

It was also those two occasions in my life as well many other scary moments of madness that opened up a different way of challenging my energy especially being in an environment I live in let alone the world we live in because it's a crazy world we live in today it's like being ignorant has become part of civilization, everywhere you look it's parents with the negligence to the kid's powers being abused by police and by other government agencies and services people getting left to their own devices people that are sleeping rough on the streets the negativity suffocates the hood and people love to keep a close eye on your movements it's like they celebrate your fails and are happy to see you struggle to get where you want to be in life but won't help you on your journey and nine times out of ten it'll be them, same people, with their hands out looking some shit when you make it out the mud.

Due to all the pain and the misery one has succumbed to from life itself I've managed to challenge that energy into a positive by doing music and also writing this book, it's not only for the reader to read about my life story but it allows me to outline the structure from being at the bottom feeling like there is no hope to getting through challenging circumstances that have made and shaped the person I have become today and also moulded to be.

Without faith, there is no hope and without hope, there is no faith so we must find it within ourselves to know that we are worthy of making a difference not only for our own lives but to many across the nation whether your an adult or a child I aim to provide the knowledge for all walks of life there should be no discrimination against age or colour.

In life, we all know that it's easy to become agitated, frustrated, and moody.

Feeling overwhelmed, like you are losing control or need to take control.

Having difficulty relaxing and quieting your mind. Feeling bad about yourself (low self-esteem), lonely, worthless, and depressed.

The word Capriciousness has both positive and negative connotations, though the negative is often the focal point since human nature tends to prefer a much more stable, predictable flow.

The occasional capricious decision and impulsive move is a welcome deviation, however. To enhance the self-healing nature of your subconscious mind, you have to practice the following tricks to remove the subconscious blocks of your life.

1. Start your day with nothing...
2. Watch your thoughts...
3. Keep yourself busy...

4. Play some relaxing music...
5. Try meditation.

Learning these exercises and having a positive attitude: Helps reduce the effects of stress, so that you can manage stress instead of stress managing you. ... Sends positive messages to the body, promoting healing. I find meditation helps me when I write because it's therapeutic enables me to overcome certain things I also think I find it's helpful within my music because it helps me get in tune with the brain, and stay focused on the right track.

Also, there are many things that I've read up on and they make a lot of sense explaining what you have to do to achieve certain things in life and I would love to share these with you so much because like I say I do not discriminate against age or colour we all bleed the same as each other, and therefore we should be willing to pass on any form of knowledge without being selfish and without withholding the information that could potentially change a persons life.

1. Make yourself necessary and you will always be needed. If you want to feel successful, learn to create, innovate or design something other people can use and need.
2. Your thoughts are like boomerangs. What you pass along to others is what will come back to you.

3. You are more defined by what comes out of your mouth than what goes in it. The way you speak and the things you say have power. Speech gives us the power to create or destroy.

4. The journey of your success will always begin with the small step of taking a chance. In business, in relationships, and in life, it all begins with a small step grounded in a desire to be better and do better.

5. Your education is never complete. Determine to live fully and continually learn. Prepare for what life has to teach by being open to the lessons in everything you do and experience.

6. Don't allow the voice of your fears to be louder than the other voices in your head. Make sure the voice of reason, the voice of belief, the voice of confidence are all strong enough to drown it out.

7. A good reputation is more valuable than money. Your reputation is built on the foundation of your character; it entails the words you speak and the actions you take. Take care of your character above all other things and your reputation will take care of itself.

8. You never really lose until you stop trying. The words I can never accomplish anything. I'll try, on the other hand, can perform wonders. Until you try you don't know what you can do.

9. You get more by giving more. Success doesn't result from how much you get but from how much you give. If you want an abundant life, give as much as you can.

10. Rule your mind or it will rule you. When you rule your mind by controlling negativity and doubt, you rule your world.

    The choice is yours to make every day.

11. Great heroes are truly humble. Most of us underrate the importance of humility. It's an important skill because it keeps you teachable, regardless of how much you already know.

12. Defeat isn't bitter if you're smart enough not to swallow it. At one time or another, we will all experience failure. The more we are willing to risk, the more we will fail. The trick is to think of failure not as the end but as part of the process.

13. Your thoughts are powerful, make them positive. To have a life that's more abundant and more successful, you must think in the limitless terms of abundance and success. Thinking is among the greatest powers we possess, and it's our choice to use it negatively or positively.

14. Forgiveness benefits two people--the giver and receiver. The bravest and the smartest thing you can do in a bad situation is to forgive and move on.

Don't allow grudges and grievances to add to the weight you carry on the road to your success.

15. The word impossible contains its opposite: "I'm possible." What impossible may be a matter of a limited point of view. Allow no limiting beliefs to restrict your outlook on life.

16. Preparation is a stepping stone to success. As the old saying goes, failing to prepare means preparing to fail. Success can be defined as being prepared.

17. You are constantly creating your reality. Your reality is built out of your thoughts, so remember how much power you have. What you think you become, what you feel you attract, what you imagine you create.

18. You are in control of your heaven or hell. You're the master of your destiny. You may not always be able to control your circumstances and environment, but how you respond is always within your control.

19. Envy consumes itself. And if you give it a foothold in your life, it will take you with it.

20. You can become bitter or better as a result of your circumstances. Your attitude is always up to you. No matter the circumstance, remind yourself that you have a choice. It's up to you to get the results you want.

21. Those who seldom make mistakes stumble upon innovation. Mistakes are proof that you're trying,

creating, exploring and discovering. Every success story, every fulfilled life needs mistakes. We may think of mistakes as meaning you've done something wrong, but in truth they mean you're doing something right.

22. It's in losing yourself that you find yourself. The greatest challenge in life is discovering who you are, and the second greatest is being happy with what you find.

23. When you're facing the right direction, all you need to do is keep walking. If you're lucky enough to know what you want, you can apply your passion and always love what you do. If you're still working to discover what you want, keep exploring. Either way, stay persistent and determined.

24. Be grateful every day, because that's the source of true power. The most important power lies in a grateful heart. Practice turning your thoughts toward appreciation and thanksgiving, because that is where you will find your gifts, strength and power.

My message in this book is essential for me to give the knowledge and to put my experiences and also the life I've lived on paper for not only my life story to be read and heard but for the knowledge and educational wisdom of life to be passed down and even though I struggle with keeping up the faith at times, it's writing this book which has made me overcome those struggles and keep the fight within me because every day is different and brings different challenges so I am still learning and reading the teachings of exercising my patience and I know the fight ain't over yet, but there's a long way to go before I've mastered the art of that teaching so I'm a keep it pushing like the hands on a clock.

Plus always remember that you can learn from others around the world both directly and indirectly.

Direct learning takes place when you ask people how they do something, listen to their answers, and try to imitate what they did. A good example is asking friends how they are going to find the time to do all the things they do, it's motivation. Sharing knowledge and insights helps people integrate information, empowers them to own their ideas, and helps them connect to new people and contexts.

The act of sharing keeps the learning alive and relevant and encourages future growth. The main reason why I did this autobiography which I hope you have enjoyed and like I said, I hope you have gained the knowledge for yourself and for you to pass it down to your loved ones many thanks to my family and true friends and the people around the world.

Signed. Aaron Nathan Grossman...

THROUGH THE EYEZ OF MINE...

CHAPTER TEN

Blessings & Appreciations.
Peace & Love.

I would like to start by giving a big thank you to my Mother Margaret Mary Marjoram for the assistance and the never-ending love and support you dearly have for your son and other kids.

This book is dedicated to you and the lost ones that we sadly miss today, you forever in my heart and it shall be written in stone and most certainly in indelible ink.

I can't thank you enough for the endless fight against our struggles and thank you for always telling me never to give up and strive for what makes me happy and try to stay positive and the best man I can be, even though days may seem harder than others we carry on and we keep it pushing.

For that reason alone I've kept those words within me and they've stuck with me through everything I've done and even though my actions on certain things may off caused you stress and anxiety it's been for a good cause to protect my family my loved ones and for those, I class as my true friends.

Not only is this book dedicated to you mum but it's to my family and the people around the world and it's a big blessing for me to give thanks once again and show my love and appreciation for those that ain't with us today. Rest in paradise to everyone that has been given their wings early and never got to fulfil their dreams and goals.

My heart still bleeds In anguish for your kids and loved ones who you sadly left behind. May the spirit of peace and harmony be with everyone as they walk through this temporary but beautiful life I pray that the life you lead brings you health and wealth plus an everlasting life of happiness.

Not only Is it my mum I would like to thank, but there are many people along the way during my time spent in the establishments of the prison system that I have so much love & respect for so if ever you read this just know I ain't forgot to mention you because I know there's still many that are not coming back home so my prayers are with you and your family.

There is just so many people to mention I'll refrain from attempting to mention everyone but all that know me throughout the prison system or in life just know it's all love and respect from the ground up and that's on my soul.

I know there's going to be a lot of people whether they are still in the system or released back out gracefully with their loved ones reading this and will come across this section of my appreciation blessings and thank yous.

Special blessings go out to all the homeboys that are sadly in the grave and are no longer with us today, my heart bleeds for your family and you'll forever be walking with us giving us the guidance and protection long live all the fallen Soulja's may your spirits bless us and guide us through hard times in this temporary but beautiful life.

I pray that everybody lives in peace and harmony because it's the fundamental prerequisite of our life and an ideal path to follow. Many ideas contribute to the logic of peace and harmony such as dealing with disputes, staying calm and focused, resolving conflicts, adjusting, adapting, neutralization, following the 'middle way' principle, etc. If people are living in harmony with each other, they are living together peacefully rather than fighting or arguing. We must try to live in peace and harmony with ourselves and those around us. It's very hard due to the violence we are exposed too so it's all about staying in tune with yourself trying to live positive.

I love all my people and everybody that I've ever come into contact with for whatever reason once a friend always a friend to me I can't thank you guys enough for taking the time out to pick up my book and I appreciate that very much.

I hope you enjoy the read and it brings you joy to flip the page and travel through my life with me; thank you for reading once again thank you very much...

Aaron Nathan Grossman.
Alias: Loczdasixth

Rest in eternal peace to all the homies and loved ones who have sadly lost their lives and have gained their wings early.

My Grandparents & Ancestors, Aunt Kate, Heart-Lou, Glouston, Martin, Erroll, Bancroft, Robert, Auntie Margaret, Paula, Chris, Leon, Miguel, Zeus, Faizal, Drè aka (BlackMagic), Luis, Clive, Jermaine, Micha, Amos, Marcus, Sasha, Karl, Gary, Bishop, Jaffa, Jackie, Dory, Warren, Ziggy, Lil-Lance, Devo, Glenny, Lil-Toddy, Liam, Kesha & Fred Wizzart & Beverly Samuels, Freddie, Dizzy, my stepdad Trevor Dailey, Donovan aka Don1, to anyone else that I haven't mentioned it's not because I've forgotten about you, it's because there is just too many people to pay homage to.

Also, rest in peace to all the families that have passed since the beginning of this pandemic...

ONCE AGAIN THANK YOU SOO MUCH TO THE WORLD & PEOPLE, FOR PURCHASING MY BOOK AND JOINING ME ALSO TAKING THE TIME OUT TO TAKE A WALK THROUGH MY LIFE JOURNEY WITH ME I APPRECIATE IT FROM THE BOTTOM OF MY HEART N SOUL!! BLESSINGS UPON BLESSINGS!!

PEACE.

Miguel Reynolds at the top. An André Marshall below him.

Martin Bennett

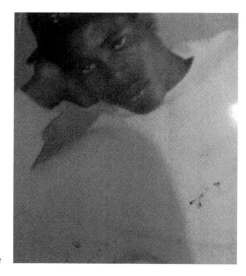

Leon Forde

Donovan Campbell

Sasha Mullings and
Martin Bennett

Emanuel, Ethline, and Daraquai Wilks

Printed in Great Britain
by Amazon

67282949R00206